To MARILYN,

A WOMAN

BRAINS, PERSONAL /FUN

A GREAT SENSE OF

AND HUMOR!

THE TRIFECTA!

Becky

START SMART,

FINISH STRONG

Forging Your Path to Operational Excellence and
Long-Term Success in the Manufacturing World

BY REBECCA MORGAN

DEDICATION

To Pete and Grandma,
who taught me to listen,
learn, and help others.

"Success is peace of mind, which is a direct result of self-satisfaction in knowing you made the effort to become the best of which you are capable."

—John Wooden

"Long ago I made this business decision: I am not here to save the world; I am here to help those who want to become great."

—Rebecca Morgan

TABLE OF
CONTENTS

INTRODUCTION

"What we have done for ourselves alone dies with us;
what we have done for others and the world remains and is
immortal."
—Albert Pike

"Share what you know. There is no other reason to know it."
—Rebecca Morgan

For over 25 years, I've helped manufacturers leverage their resources—their cash, their people, and their capabilities—to be more successful. Along the way, I've discovered that most manufacturers are good enough at many aspects of their business, but surprisingly few are excellent at what matters most. In fact, all manufacturers can still do better at their most critical competencies. And they need to. Due to increasingly rapid globalization and heightened competition in the industry, it's no longer an option not to.

Despite constant rumbling in the media that "manufacturing is dead," it's not. Far from it. Manufacturing will never be dead—of that I'm certain. However, it's true that the nature of manufacturing, such as where and how it's done, is continually evolving. Any manufacturer who doesn't move forward quickly, and with a commitment to excellence, is in danger of falling behind the curve, and being left in the dust.

This book is for those manufacturing executives who are determined not to be left behind. It's for any manufacturer who seeks excellence; who wants to learn and grow; and who's willing to adapt and change in order to achieve long-term business success.

To that end, Start Smart, Finish Strong is a collection of practical strategies that any manufacturer will benefit from following. As you implement the strategies inside these pages at your organization, a better, more sustainable future will emerge for you and all your stakeholders—employees, customers, suppliers, investors, and the community at large.

I wrote Start Smart, Finish Strong to share my expertise with as many people as possible—to help as many manufacturers as I can. I sincerely hope the following pages inspire a transformation at your organization.

To excellence and long-term success,

Rebecca Morgan

President
Fulcrum ConsultingWorks, Inc.

CHAPTER 1:
LEARNING TO LEAD

"I know that I will work hard and give it my all.
I just hope to be part of a good team."
—Andee Whitaker

"The vast majority of employees feel the same way.
Help them reach that goal, and you'll reach yours."
—Rebecca Morgan

It's no coincidence that the first chapter of this book is about leadership. Leadership in manufacturing is just as important as it is in any other industry. That is to say, it can be the difference between a good organization and an exceptional one.

And in many ways, leadership in manufacturing is more difficult than it is in other businesses. In large part, that's because manufacturing is constantly undergoing major changes due to globalization, technology advances, and political swings.

Manufacturing has been frequently transformed by the opening up of new markets, and new options for low-cost labor. Factors such as low labor rates in China or Vietnam's growing textile skills affect manufacturers everywhere. This type of globalization makes the natural demands of manufacturing that much more challenging.

As a result, manufacturing leaders can't just focus internally. They must focus externally as well. They must know what their companies do well internally—but they must also be aware of the worldwide environment, pioneering technologies, progress in material science, socioeconomic issues, and other areas outside their own isolated organization.

Now, many manufacturing leaders are good leaders. But many of them still have to overcome one destructive misconception that's shared among all too many manufacturing executives: **Leaders know everything. Employees know nothing.**

As an industry, manufacturing has been operating under this assumption for almost a century. To thrive in today's market and effectively face globalization, manufacturing leaders must shift their thinking. They must realize that everyone—not just the C-suite—can contribute to making an organization great. And everyone should.

This new outlook on success in manufacturing, one in which every employee is integral to achieving company goals, must be incorporated into the way leaders behave at all times. In this chapter, you'll learn eight key strategies to strengthen your leadership approach in just this way, raising up your entire company along with you.

STRATEGY #1:

BUILD A GREAT TEAM

I'm a sports fanatic—especially when it comes to college basketball and March Madness. Every year, I faithfully fill out my bracket. And like most, my bracket is often busted on the first Thursday of the tournament, and blown apart by the end of that first weekend.

What does March Madness have to do with successful leadership in manufacturing? As it turns out, quite a lot. Over the years, it's become increasingly obvious to me that success in sports is closely tied to success in the manufacturing C-suite. What it takes to lead a basketball team to a championship trophy is remarkably similar to what it takes to lead a manufacturing company to long-term success.

To start, there are three key takeaways from the world of sports that every business leader should pay attention to:

1. Great teams can beat great players. They don't always, but they frequently do. And a great team with a few great players who understand their roles? Unstoppable. The crucial point here is that you should focus on developing a cohesive team of skilled employees. Don't invest all your time and energy in developing just one or two superstars at your company. In order for your most talented employees to reach their full potential, they'll need the support of a competent, dedicated team behind them.

2. Great teams have excellent coaches. Not many of us would be willing to have our professional futures depend on the performance of a bunch of 17 to 21-year-old kids who've been told how great they are since birth. It can't be easy to get the attention of those young men, convince them to trust their teammates, and persuade them to focus on team success over individual performance. But the best basketball coaches do just that. These coaches give and demand respect, listen and convince, and—above all—select players with the skills needed for team success. That's exactly the kind of leader the manufacturing business requires.

3. Experience counts, but only for so much.

Back in 2014, the Final 4 involved two teams with coaches who were completely new to that pressure-cooker environment. Great coaches can lead through unfamiliar circumstances by putting players in a position to succeed, and by focusing on what's familiar over what's different. After all, it's still basketball, even if it's the Final 4. Likewise, a good manufacturing executive can successfully navigate unfamiliar circumstances by relying on good business instincts, supporting employees, and identifying all "known factors."

Just as a great basketball team won't win every single game of the season, your company won't win over every single potential customer. Customers' decisions to do business with you—or not—are an agglomeration of "one and done" business decisions. You won't win every one, but you must win enough of them to be in the tournament every year.

To accomplish that, build a team that's focused more on overall success than individual records, led by coaches who know how to lead in both familiar and unfamiliar circumstances. And don't think for a minute that your incumbent role can't be overcome by the new kid on the block.

STRATEGY #2:

EMBRACE A COACH'S MINDSET

For many business executives, viewing themselves as "coaches" can require a major shift in thinking. So before you can effectively lead your team to victory, you must understand what it means to be a good coach. How can we tell an excellent coach from a mediocre or bad one?

A coach exists to help develop skills, situational awareness, and thinking and behavioral practices that facilitate success. A good coach knows what questions to ask, and when to ask them (more on that in Strategy #3). A good coach ensures the "student" clearly understands the objective and the strategy for reaching it, knows what behaviors will increase success, and respects the student's potential. A good coach knows that results can reflect luck, but great coaching will ensure continued success.

"Don Shula can take his'n and beat your'n," said Bum Phillips, then the NFL Houston Oilers coach. "Or he can take your'n and beat his'n." Now there's a good coach, and a good standard to consider when evaluating your own coaching skills. Do the people you coach consistently reach their full potential? Do they know how to win?

As you prepare to flex your coaching muscles, make sure your employees are operating as a true team. Too many people rely on years of elapsed time—or "past experience"—to build and strengthen a team. However, there are three practical approaches that will grow your team member capability much more quickly:

1. Have your top two performers switch jobs.
They will each learn new skills, stretch their capabilities, and inject fresh thinking into the work environment. If you're afraid to do this, ask yourself why. There's a problem to be solved.

2. Ask your team members to "self-score." Using any of the number of widely available "excellence award" applications, ask your team members to self-score—and then discuss their reasoning. This sharing of views will create cross-functional awareness, thinking, and goal alignment that can only be valuable for the team-development process.

3. Require a weeklong "recess" for each team member.

Every year, require each member of your leadership team to take one week away from the office just to read, write, and think. No checking emails, no answering the phone. This weeklong recess from work is a powerful way to stimulate new perspectives and ideas. It's also a great development opportunity for the individual assigned to fill that person's work role for the week.

Working at the same job every day can create myopic thinking and boredom, even for top executives. A sponsored break to refresh the mind can create a re-invigorated leader; that rarely happens from family vacations.

When creating a team to accomplish a task, plan time for them to get to know one another, discuss roles and responsibilities, and agree on operating guidelines. And remember: No matter how smart, how experienced, or how caring they are as individuals, they will not suddenly become a team just because the game has started.
A little creativity goes a long way in coaching a great team. Don't get stuck waiting for time to pass.

STRATEGY #3:

ASK QUESTIONS—
DON'T DEMAND ANSWERS

Contrary to popular belief, great leaders don't have all the answers—but they do ask the best questions. The best coaches develop strong thinking skills in team members, all by stimulating the right kind of conversation.

With that in mind, have you ever said to your employees, "Don't bring me a problem unless you also bring me a solution"? This is a relatively common management philosophy, intended to create accountability among employees. But there are two significant downsides to this leadership approach.

First, it encourages employees to delay bringing attention to problems. Second, when employees do acknowledge a problem, it encourages them to suggest the first solution that comes to mind. Employees can usually develop better solutions to problems than management can, if only because they're closer to the issue. Speed is important, but developing a solution that will actually solve the problem—and not merely apply a Band-Aid—is more important.

As the leader of your company, it's up to you to make problems a comfortable part of the conversation. A few easy questions can ensure that a valid problem-solving culture is developed, from the top down:

1. "What evidence do you have that you've correctly identified the problem?" We all have opinions, but they bring little value. We need facts. Yes, education improves thinking, but its downside is making us think we know more than we do. As an effective business leader, it's your job to insist on facts, not anecdotal stories or opinions.

2. "What other options did you consider?" Ask this question as you discuss the employee's recommended solution. Many of us jump to conclusions. The odds of jumping to the best and most permanent solution straightaway are poor. By forcing the consideration of two or three different options, you'll help your team develop better solutions.

3. "What did we learn?" This last question can be asked at any stage of problem-solving, but it's best to ask it after the selected countermeasure has been implemented. Most people don't think about learning. They're only concerned with making the bleeding stop. This is your opportunity to force thinking and capture learning.

There's always more than one approach to solve a problem—and the coach's initial approach might not be the best one. Always listen, question, reinforce learning from failure, and take great pride in the development of your team members. Don't simply demand answers.

//

Contrary to popular belief, great leaders don't have all the answers — but they do ask the best questions."

STRATEGY #4:

DON'T WASTE TIME ON CONSENSUS

An authoritarian leadership style was once considered the only way to effectively lead a business. Not so anymore. As the "command and control" organizational structure has fallen out of favor, some believe that consensus is the replacement leadership model. Let me tell you: It's not.

In fact, finding consensus is best limited to innocuous situations. Just because Think about it: Do you really want your employees to vote on strategy? On which bank to use? On pricing? On which markets to penetrate next? Asking for input is one thing; waiting for consensus to build is just wasting time. The key is to strike the right balance between authority and respect for your team.

With a common vision, mission, and set of core values, leaders and followers can accomplish amazing things together. But first, there must be mutual respect, regardless of company position. There must be leaders who listen, and who respect decisions made by followers. And there must be followers who listen, and who respect decisions made by leaders.

While sharing opinions is valuable to learning, building consensus can be paralyzing for an organization. Getting everyone to agree before taking action is the surest way not to take action. Leadership is not a popularity contest: It's based on the confidence and support of followers. Spend your time building that, not consensus.

The most effective way to build support from your followers is to admit that you don't know everything. Once leaders become vulnerable, then they can be seen as human. Only then can they be trusted. If you pretend that you don't make mistakes, the people who work for you won't trust you. People want to follow a strong leader—but being strong and being vulnerable are not incompatible leadership qualities.

Open yourself up to your employees, managers, and fellow executives. Let them see your human side, and their confidence in you will grow.

//
Leadership is not a popularity contest: It's based on the confidence and support of followers."

STRATEGY #5:

BE CARING and PERSISTENT

I've had the honor of walking through hundreds of manufacturing operations over the years. In every one of them, I learned something new—if only how not to do something. In most, I observed a number of great ideas and useful behaviors.

From those experiences—and from spending nearly three decades working with client companies committed to improving—I've come to recognize two key leadership behaviors that set the best manufacturing organizations apart from the rest:

1. Caring. The concept of caring might sound simple, but it's exceedingly difficult for most executives to get it right. Why? Because you have to actually care. High-quality organizations care about their employee families, their business partners, their communities, and the broader future. As a result, their leaders act, think, and operate with others in mind—a behavior trait that gives these companies a tremendous competitive advantage.

A commitment to safety is one of the best signs of a caring company culture. Another sure sign is when leaders are committed to developing employee skillsets. If you truly care about your employees, then you're more than happy to help them pay for their continued development— and let them take courses on company time. A developing employee is not separate from a good employee.

Sure, we all get mad or frustrated, even with those we care about. Sometimes tough love is required. But an owner or executive can't move an organization forward alone. Lasting success requires that all stakeholders move forward together. Meaningful success continues generation after generation. It doesn't end after 20 or 30 years.

It's true that, with enough money, an abusive organization can survive for a century. Maybe even longer. However, in time, companies that only care about the bottom line will always collapse. That's why caring is one of the most essential qualities a business leader can possess.

2. Persistence. Organizations that hop from one flavor of the month to the next will eventually burn out. It's exhausting for everyone when business leaders are indecisive, quick to abandon plans, and unable to stick to their ideas. This isn't to say that leaders shouldn't look outside the organization for new ideas and better strategies—certainly they should. But once you identify the appropriate operating model for your company, be persistent with it. And teach your managers and team members to do the same.

Persistence is strictly a function of focus and priority. As executives, we get torn in hundreds of different directions. It's easy to lose sight of top priorities. But leaders must be committed personally to the goals they want their employees to achieve. Lack of persistence is typically the result of too many priorities, and failure to reinforce key goals.

In manufacturing, the companies who lead the pack have developed a philosophy of improvement, and they're persistent with it. Activity failures are common, but they're also the basis of becoming a learning organization. Strong leaders recognize that. Being persistent means not being thwarted by minor failures, or even major ones. It means constantly working to improve your results, without sacrificing the principles of the strategy you've chosen.

//

High-quality organizations are both persistent and caring."

As the leader of your business, it's your responsibility to foster a culture of caring and persistence throughout the ranks. With a caring and persistent leader at the helm, your organization will steadily improve over time, following the direction you set forth.

Keep in mind that persistence is wasted if you have a single-minded focus on day-to-day issues—to the exclusion of your long-term contribution to the betterment of mankind. Always remember that it's not enough just to be persistent. High-quality organizations are both persistent and caring. Consider your company's impact on the world. Strive to develop an environment of consistency and determination to give your employees their best shot at being successful.

STRATEGY #6:

ASSESS THREATS AND OPPORTUNITIES

Everyone knows it's an executive's job to help organizations identify threats, fix weaknesses, build on strengths, and find opportunities for success. The real challenge is figuring out how to do so in an organized, effective, and repeatable way. For decades, MBA programs have pushed several "management tools" that claim to solve this common problem. I'm here to tell you: Beware.

While it's easy to accept existing and well-documented management tools as productive—especially when they're touted by respectable MBA programs—it's nearly impossible to determine how helpful they actually are. In reality, some of the most popular management tools out there aren't just unhelpful; they're downright destructive.

To assess threats and opportunities in a way that truly helps your organization, you can start by avoiding these three widespread approaches:

1. The traditional SWOT analysis. Many companies complete an annual SWOT (Strengths, Weaknesses, Opportunities, Threats) analysis as part of the strategic planning process. Every MBA graduate knows how to create the four-box square, with strengths and weaknesses in the left two boxes and opportunities and threats in the right two. And any executive can quickly document the top four to six items in each box.

Why is this approach so easy and fast? Because too often it states the obvious—and then states it again. Strengths are rephrased as opportunities. Weaknesses are rephrased as threats. And we're done. Have we added any in-depth understanding of our business? No. We might pretend we have, but this "management tool" tells us nothing that we didn't already know.

2. Management by Objectives (MBOs). Why are MBOs so popular? Again, because they're easy. An executive can simply give each of his direct reports a handful of metrics to hit, or a few projects to finish, and then send them on their way. This delivers a "by any means necessary" message to the entire team, eliminating much of the nuance needed in management strategy.

This goal-setting management approach puts a tremendous amount of pressure on employees. It can be difficult for managers and employees to accurately prioritize short-term and long-term projects, leading to disorganization. And it rarely reflects consistent thinking or priorities across company departments. I know your organization is better than that.

3. "Stack ranking." This approach is similar to Jack Welch's famous "get rid of the bottom 10% annually" mentality. Stack ranking goes by many names, but it's simply a method by which each department head is forced to rank his direct reports from top to bottom.

What are the chances that every department has the exact same mean and standard deviation in its hiring, development, and performance measurements? Zero. Stack ranking is just an easy—but lazy—way to get rid of people. Unfortunately, if you use this management approach, you'll end up getting rid of many good people, and find it difficult to keep those remaining.

So don't fall prey to blindly trusting the top Google hits for "management techniques." Just because Fortune 500 companies do something, that doesn't mean it makes sense.

Instead, you should honestly examine the management techniques you use. Do they make your organization a better company? Do those involved recognize the value they add? And what are some alternatives that might work better for you?

As everyone's mother once warned: "Just because your friends jump in the lake doesn't mean you should too!" Opportunities and threats are there for all of us. We just have to look around, and be willing to manage the risks that come with progress.

STRATEGY #7:

DON'T ISOLATE YOURSELF

Long, long ago, I was employed by several large companies. I had been raised to work hard, so I did. I focused on learning everything about my employers' businesses, and took every opportunity to learn from fellow employees.

Sounds responsible so far, doesn't it? But while working for those companies, I rarely glanced out the windows or opened the doors to learn what everyone else in the world was doing.

Luckily, I worked for some high-caliber organizations, so the learningwas valuable, even if internally focused. When I chose to walk out those "employee" doors forever in 1990, I found an exciting, fast-paced, ever-changing world around me.

As the owner of my own consulting business for over 25 years, I've had the joy of learning more every few weeks than I ever did in six months as an employee. I'm no more curious now than I was before; I'm just more focused on looking outward as I learn every day.

You don't have to run your own business to learn from everyone; you simply have to look externally more frequently. Find people who are smarter than you, who think differently than you. Listen and learn. Don't isolate yourself. Expose yourself to the outside world.

One of the best ways to find external guidance, inspiration, and knowledge is to work with a coach. All extremely successful professionals want help in maximizing performance. Certainly every renowned athlete uses at least one trainer, and most work with several specialists. Actors and singing stars use coaches, too.

A recent study found that, unfortunately, only a third of CEOs in the United States work with a coach. That same study found that the vast majority of CEOs want a coach. One has to wonder: If so many business executives want external help, why do so few actually get it? And why do so many employees, supervisors, managers, and executives insist they "know" the facts when they're really voicing opinions or experience-based guesses?

Motivation, money, and vulnerability are requirements of anyone working with external professional experts. For me, vulnerability was the most difficult of those to meet. When I worked as a corporate executive, it seemed risky to

As a consultant, I've come to recognize just how silly that is. None of us knows everything—and all of us can benefit from outside expertise. There's a huge difference between the arrogance that one knows everything and the confidence that one can learn anything.

There's nothing wrong with opinions or guesses, except when they get in the way of discovering the facts. Facts are how we learn, drive out problems, and succeed. Experience, education, and critical thinking skills can enable discovery, but only through hypothesis-testing and a willingness to admit we don't know everything. If calling yourself "ignorant" feels harsh, at least be willing to admit, "I don't yet have the facts required to truly understand the problem, but I'll work to get them." Be comfortable saying, "Help me understand." Everyone will learn more.

Here's a personal story that illustrates the power of asking for help. As an undergraduate studying economics, I took a graduate class in European history because it was in the right building at the right time. I was thoroughly unprepared.

I'll never forget the feeling of being completely lost, not sure if the professor was talking about countries, people, religions, or something else entirely. I took notes phonetically and then spent evenings trying to figure out what it all meant.

What I couldn't figure out, I'd ask about before the next class. I earned an A, but would have flunked without the willingness to admit how much I didn't know, both to myself and to the professor. We're all ignorant in many arenas, even those we've spent years seeking to master. Ignorant is not a dirty word. It's the first step in learning. Those who pretend to know everything can't grow.

I've worked with coaches in many aspects of my personal and business development over the past two decades, and my clients are the beneficiaries of that. I learn more every day now than I did in a month in my corporate life. That wasted time is my fault. I could have hired outside expertise, even if it required spending my own money.

If you're approaching the end of your career, remember how an aging and limping Kirk Gibson rounded the bases to win Game 1 of the 1988 World Series for the Dodgers. He had continued working with hitting coaches right up to his walk to the plate in the bottom of the ninth with two outs. His game-winning home run is now unforgettable history. If you're earlier in your career, don't make the foolish mistake I did of believing outside expertise was a sign of weakness. To the contrary, it's a sign of commitment to greatness.

STRATEGY #8:

FINISH WHAT YOU START

I've long been struck by the failure of most manufacturing companies to actually finish what they start—ergo, my trademarked concept, Finish Strong®. I came up with this concept after years of working with client companies who wanted to improve. It effectively summarizes what exceptional companies do differently, what sets them apart from the competition.

In short, they don't leave loose ends hanging around. They dot their I's, they cross their T's. They make sure they cross the finish line before they go on to the next thing. The Finish Strong® name describes it perfectly. Here's a visual of the process itself:

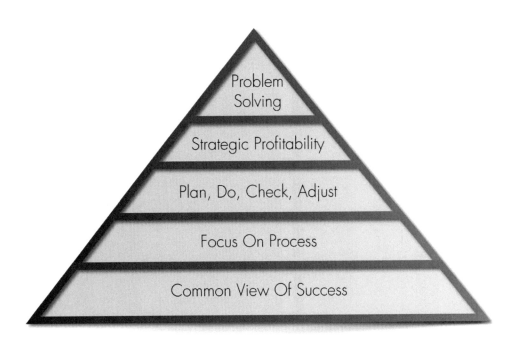

The Finish Strong® Path To Profitability

I simply can't bear to see companies fail to finish what they start, squandering opportunities to stay ahead of the competition. Why do so many manufacturers demonstrate this weakness?

Common causes include a lack of process to create management focus, unwillingness to make difficult prioritization decisions, and a delusional belief that "delegation" means "done." Just because you tell someone to do something, doesn't mean they will. Just because you follow up to verify that they took action, doesn't mean the action will stick.

Of course, you have a lot on your plate. But so do your employees—you put most of it there. Your employees aren't irresponsible; they try to accomplish what they believe you see as important. If their impression of your priorities changes frequently, or if they perceive them to be too numerous to successfully address, they'll bring little or nothing to completion in trying to do some of everything.

As the leader of your organization, it's your job to refocus your team and ensure everyone finishes what they start. So let's walk through the elements of Finish Strong® thinking. Companies who successfully integrate these behaviors stand head and shoulders above those who don't. Finish Strong® incorporates five key elements:

1. A common view of success. Before you do anything
else, you must create a common and consistent view of success across your company. Some people refer to this as the "true north" for an organization. The key is to make sure that everyone has the same view of what will make your company successful. Differences of opinion here can cripple an organization.

2. Focus on process. The next step is to focus on process.
Without the right process, you can't lead your organization to achieve your common view of success. Executing the right processes well will produce the results you want.

3. Plan, do, check, adjust. Once you have the process
in place, it's time to build a strong plan. This might sound easy, but it requires patience and discipline: Build a plan, do it, check it, and then adjust it. This is how you create an organization that's constantly learning, focused, and moving in the right direction.

4. Strategic profitability. The three elements above create an incredibly strong foundation. Now it's time to assimilate strategic profitability into your organizational decision making. By integrating concepts from theory of constraints, lean, and the science of economics, strategic profitability supports effective management of bottlenecks and complexity. **You'll learn more about strategic profitability in Strategy #12: Don't Maximize Profits—Strategize Them.**

5. Problem solving. The fifth aspect of Finish Strong® is to develop the problem-solving skills of all your employees. The goal here is to teach your employees how to drive repeat problems out of the business forever. In Chapter 6: Problem Solving and Improving, you'll learn key strategies to create a successful problem-solving culture at your company.

I'm proud to say that my best clients have used the Finish Strong® concept to achieve dramatic results and competitive advantage. Consider how you can use this transformational process to help your organization execute better than your competition, time and time again.

CHAPTER 2:
YOUR STRATEGIC VISION

"Efforts and courage are not enough without purpose
and direction."
—John Fitzerald Kennedy

"The leader must make both purpose and direction
clear."
—Rebecca Morgan

Some people think manufacturing is about making products, pure and simple. But at its core, manufacturing is actually a service business—one that happens to involve making products. That's why you can't achieve long-term success without a strategic vision that goes beyond your products.

Your strategic vision is what enables you to truly understand the business you're in. It clarifies your organization's role in the industry, identifies the capabilities required to provide excellent service to your customers, and keeps you outwardly focused. A strong strategic vision also defines how your products fit into your target market—both today, and far into the future.

With a strong strategic vision, you'll never be caught unaware by changes in the marketplace. Instead, you'll always know where and how your products and capabilities fit into every industry change, big or small.

In short, your strategic vision is a clear notion of who you are as a company. Once you've established a strategic vision, you'll be better equipped to choose the best strategies for your organization. In fact, using the right strategies is key to leveraging your strategic vision for competitive advantage. The big challenge is that you need to start thinking strategically—not tactically, as the vast majority of manufacturing executives do.

Many CEOs and COOs at midmarket companies fail to think strategically because they don't look far enough into the future. How far in the future can you see? If the answer is less than six months, then you're in deep trouble.

The key to building your strategic vision is to think ahead, and then filter that thinking into your vision of what the organization needs to do—and what it needs to be—for continued success.

The following six strategies are designed to help you develop and leverage your own strategic vision in the manufacturing business. You'll learn to get strategically ahead of market changes—so you can preemptively figure out how to support your business—instead of just reacting to them. Let's get started.

STRATEGY #9:

ELIMINATE YOUR BLIND SPOTS

Many years ago, the automotive industry began concentrating on designing safe vehicles. For most of them, that meant seat belts, air bags, and bumpers that absorbed energy from a straight-on crash. But Toyota, which has long held the goal of manufacturing a completely safe vehicle, didn't just focus on minimizing damage from a collision. Instead, Toyota's engineers asked, "How can we prevent an accident from happening in the first place?"

Many of Toyota's competitors were flummoxed by the challenge of driver-caused crashes. After all, it seemed far-fetched that a car company could prevent drivers from making mistakes that lead to a wreck.

Now, just look at the state of automobile safety today: We have cars with backup cameras, automatic parking, and even automatic braking. By focusing on the kinds of mistakes drivers make, and working to eliminate those causes, the automotive industry is steadily moving toward that once-elusive goal of a completely safe vehicle.

No matter what type of manufacturing you're in, this lesson from the car industry is crucial to developing your strategic vision. If cars can be designed to overcome the mistakes of drivers, what can your product be designed to accomplish that no one thinks it can?

As you consider your products and your markets, think about the various assumptions you make that might be limiting your innovation. Figure out what's blocking the creativity of your team. By eliminating these "blind spots" you can create value that others can't even conceive—and clarify the direction of your company.

Unfortunately, many manufacturing executives are caught in what I call the "fog of familiarity" at their organizations. It's the reason why an outside consultant can walk into an organization and see in just minutes what a CEO hasn't been able to see for months. Put simply, outside consultants are immune to the fog that clouds the vision of people inside the company.

To clear the fog within your organization for a stronger strategic vision, use these three powerful tactics:

1. Observe. While it might feel awkward at first, I encourage you to stand in one place at your company—and simply watch. Watch the way your organization operates. Watch for safety issues. Watch for wasted time. Watch until you find yourself asking, "Why do we do that?" or "Why do we do that that way?" If you're not yet seeing things that don't make sense, then you haven't been watching long enough.

2. Challenge assumptions. Assumptions are some of the most dangerous threats to your business. Wrong assumptions can mean lost profits, bad decisions, and misguided strategies. It's important to challenge the assumptions at your company, both spoken and unspoken. Ask yourself questions such as, "Is that the best location for that piece of equipment? Do we really need to three-way match every invoice? And why is scheduling located in the offices rather than on the floor?"

3. Keep asking questions. As you might have noticed, asking questions is a critical part of "clearing the fog" at your organization. The importance of asking questions simply can't be overstated. When the responses to your questions indicate a real lack of understanding as to why, how, or when, you must begin to dig deeper. It's the only real way to avoid the "we've always done it this way!" fog that clouds your strategic vision.

STRATEGY #10:

KEEP AN EYE ON CORE PRIORITIES

Shoeless Joe Jackson betrayed the baseball world by participating in the famed "Black Sox Scandal" in the 1919 World Series. This great baseball player let the other team win. His betrayal was so great that I grew up thinking no one in sports would ever cheat again. Then came Sosa, McGuire, and Charlie Hustle. SMU and Miami college football. Lance Armstrong. In sports of all kinds, it's easier today to presume duplicity than honest talent.

Jeff Skilling, Dennis Kozlowski, and Bernie Madoff might be the poster boys for unethical businessmen, but there are plenty more where they came from. Just look for the "too good to be true" headlines and, as Watergate's Deep Throat said, "Follow the money."

Although these corrupt behaviors seem pervasive, cheating and fraud are less likely to beleaguer your company's strategic vision than a simple lack of focus.

You read that right. A simple lack of focus can do just as much to derail your company from achieving its strategic vision as old-fashioned fraud can—and it's far more likely to happen. As a business leader, you must take focus just as seriously as fraud prevention.

Your team is likely honest, hard-working, and committed. But your employees might also be working on the wrong things, despite knowing the company's priorities. Before your organization begins to swirl down the drain and you're left wondering how it happened, have the discipline to regularly verify your team's key areas of actual work. In other words, keep your eye on core priorities.

The dictionary definition of priority is "something given or meriting attention before competing alternatives." Just how many priorities can your team successfully address at any one time? And how can you be sure that what's given attention is what merits attention before competing alternatives?

Leaders are responsible for positioning their people for success. That requires making the critical choices—establishing specific priorities for everyone. You can make better decisions and achieve more alignment in your organization if you set priorities on your own, limiting the range of decisions others can make. Don't just give your team a laundry list of items to work on. This gives them the responsibility to choose priorities and dilutes the importance of everything on the list. Instead, be specific about priorities and keep tabs on their progress. Not to micromanage, but to ensure distractions are not interfering with what is truly important.

//

Leaders are responsible for positioning their people for success."

As you determine core priorities for your team, benchmarking is an important tool to master. This is the valuable practice of comparing your business processes and performance metrics to others. Effective benchmarking is a powerful way to ensure you're focusing on the right priorities to improve your organization and fulfill your strategic vision. Unfortunately, the majority of manufacturers execute benchmarking ineffectively. Here's how to do it well:

1. Have specific goals in mind. Effective benchmarking is always begun with a specific goal in mind. If you don't have a well-defined reason to benchmark something, then it's not truly benchmarking. Simply going to visit another manufacturing operation is not a benchmarking activity. True benchmarking is done with specific intent, and it's mutually beneficial for you and the company that's hosting you. It's your responsibility to ensure the exchange meets that requirement.

2. Benchmark with the best. Benchmarking can be done with anyone, but I encourage you to benchmark with the best companies you can find—not just companies like yours in industries similar to yours. Identifying the best organizations to benchmark with can take time, and it certainly requires effort. However, it's well worth it to benchmark your organization's processes against those of a company who leads the pack in an area important to your competitive advantage.

3. Discuss metrics in advance. Regardless of which area you intend to benchmark, prepare beforehand by discussing metrics with your host. Another company's 100% on-time performance may be inferior to your 80% performance, depending on how the metric is defined. As you become aware of the host company's performance metrics for areas that interest you, begin to develop your discussion list. You'll undoubtedly have questions, as will they. Some examples of topics to discuss might be the evolution of their metrics over time, what they believe to be most important to their achievement level, and which metrics are specific to the area being examined.

4. Benchmark internally, too. Ideas about excellence come from both internal and external sources—neither is sufficient alone. If you have more safety incidents in some areas of your operation than others, require your team to benchmark internally to learn company best practices. In lean manufacturing, that spreading of internal best practices is called yokaten; everywhere else it's called doing what makes sense. Encourage your employees to observe, listen, and share.

Requiring benchmarking, establishing priorities, and ensuring they're given precedence isn't micromanaging. It's simply the act of ensuring common criteria for decision-making whenever a decision matters, knowing what merits attention first, and reinforcing that message regularly. That's what I call fulfilling your strategic vision.

STRATEGY #11:

THINK STRATEGICALLY, NOT TACTICALLY

When it comes to the way we think, most of us were brought up on the tactical side of the manufacturing business. The vast majority of operations people are used to the "whatever it takes" mantra—the "get order, fill order" mentality. The reality is, this mindset costs a fortune; it's simply not profitable. As a direct result of this tactical way of thinking, most small to mid-sized manufacturers don't have an operations strategy—at all.

To ensure that your organization is set on a strategic path, you must transition your own way of thinking from tactical to strategic. Instead of "let's do whatever it takes," your mindset should be "let's figure out what it's going to take to do this repeatedly, reliably, and profitably."

Let's start by talking about what "strategic" actually means. Strategy is a word that everyone knows, but not many people truly understand. Executives tend to take it as a criticism when they're told that they aren't strategic thinkers—but it's not intended to offend. Recognizing that you're not a strategic thinker is the first step to becoming one.

The best way to explain the difference between strategic and tactical thinking is to give you an example. Pretend you're planning to open a distribution center. You can either say right away, "Hey, we've got a bunch of sales going on in Europe. Let's put the distribution center in Germany." Or, you can say, "I know we're starting to emphasize international growth. But do we want to supply the market from the United States? And if we want to supply the market from somewhere in Europe, what are the transportation considerations? What are the legal and labor considerations? Do we want to finish the product there, or do we want to ship the finished product there, house it, and then distribute it?"

The first approach is a tactical way of thinking. The decision to put the distribution center in Germany is a one-off decision, separate from any discussion about overall company direction. On the other hand, the second approach is strategic. Instead of making a one-off decision, certain guidelines and protocols are discussed and mulled over before coming to a conclusion.

Strategy is all about defining these types of guidelines. As a strategic thinker, you can determine how you want to approach decisions so that, in the future, all of your decisions are made within the context of the same strategy. Clear strategy is a prerequisite of making good decisions.

Now that you know what strategic thinking is, it's time to be honest with yourself. Are you thinking strategically right now? If not, it's time to start. As a strategic thinker, you'll be able to align your operations with your strategic vision and ultimately lead your company to more profitability.

STRATEGY #12:

DON'T MAXIMIZE PROFITS— STRATEGIZE THEM

Business owners and executives care about profitability, as they should. Profitability pays the bills and makes the future possible. But just as not all markets are good markets, not all customers are good customers, and not all orders are good orders, the same is true for profits. Not all profits are good profits.

How can that be? Some profits cost you more than they're worth, and are realized by actions inconsistent with your strategic vision. Traditional profits are the profits—or "the bottom line"—that you've long been familiar with. Meanwhile, strategic profits are designed to achieve a more targeted goal than simply maximizing profits at all costs. And that goal is closely aligned with the organization's strategic vision.

More and more organizations have a goal much larger than making money. The majority of privately held manufacturing companies want to make the world a better place. Goals and visions vary widely. Some have a goal of creating new technologies or providing jobs. Others are committed to handing down the company from one generation to the next. Some businesses want to solve a major worldwide challenge, like unclean drinking water. Reaching those goals may not involve maximizing profits today or in the future.

//
Not all profits are good profits."

"Thinking strategic profits" is the process of strategizing profits in order to attain your goal, whatever it may be. In this process, it's important to clearly define your personal concept of business success, understand your options for attaining it, and create the environment that sustains it over time. This is the process of maximizing your strategic profits, instead of merely regular profits. Defining your unwavering view of what business success creates is the first step in maximizing strategic profits. Thinking strategic profits reflects a coherent body of intentional vital decisions about, among other things,

- Your definition of business success
- Your choice of excellence partners
- Your resource and capability development
- Your opportunity costs
- Complexity

Every choice has consequences, some short-term and others over a longer horizon, and each is made in a context that may be of short or long-term duration. Should your company work with a domestic customer that wants you to expand internationally to support one of their foreign operations? Should you meet the competition's price on a large potential order? Is agreeing to supply that large corporation with custom products the right decision? Should your team work overtime to get an order out that the customer really wants now? It depends. Where are you trying to go, what are your options, and where are you now?

Why are strategic profits worth your time and energy? Because smaller profits aren't necessarily bad, and higher profits aren't necessarily good; it all depends on the environment you envision resulting from business success. In other words, not all profits are aligned with your strategic vision—and it's worth your time and energy to focus on those that are.

Discover more about this process by reading my free e-book Strategic Profits, available through my website, WWW.FULCRUMCWI.COM

STRATEGY #13:

LEVERAGE EXECUTIVE ACTIONS

In 2015, Apple and IBM developed an iPad specifically for senior citizens. It might not sound like the coolest product, but it targeted a rapidly growing demographic. This new iPad was first released in Japan—another large market. Most would agree that this product was a worthwhile effort, taking advantage of a clear market opportunity.

Meanwhile, apartments in downtown Cleveland, Ohio, have a 98 percent occupancy rate, with a six-month waitlist. Residents are a mix of young and old. One might think this bustling area of Ohio would be a great market for selling cars. But these downtown apartments are filled with people who love to walk, bike, and live in the heart of the city. Trying to sell cars to them would be more difficult than trying to sell ice cream in the winter. It can be done—but is it worth the effort? Most would agree not.

These two vastly different examples illustrate one key point: While some market-defining attributes are predictable, many are not. As the leader of your organization, it's your job to ensure that the best markets are identified—and entered successfully. One of the best ways to do that is to leverage several executive actions to align marketing and operations.

Let me explain. In manufacturing, marketing is typically responsible for considering demographics, economic outlook, and geopolitical activities to assess market opportunities. Marketing will work with operations, too, and consider any evolving or potential technologies.

As soon as marketing identifies a profitable opportunity, operations is expected to be ready to deliver. But without a clear strategy to align the two departments, it can all fall apart. As you establish a strategic vision that prepares you for changing market needs, you must align marketing and operations to accurately determine which markets to pursue. That's where your executive actions come in.

Leverage these executive actions to closely align marketing and operations, and anticipate changing market needs:

1. Hold monthly strategic meetings with marketing and operations.
Under your guidance, marketing and operations leadership should meet once a month to discuss what they're seeing in current markets. At their core, these meetings provide powerful input to the traditional sales and operations planning process. Without this high-level vision and analysis, sales and operations can easily denigrate into myopic, "more of the same" decision making. With the help of your executive strategic meetings, both sales and operations leaders will broaden their outlook and be better prepared for market changes.

Keep in mind that monthly meetings can be a giant waste of time if they're not well-planned and orchestrated. To make this monthly meeting effective, you must do two things: identify the right levels of participation, and instill the discipline of an agenda to ensure that participants gather the right kinds of information from the right sources. The output of this meeting is a collaborative strategic decision about how the information will be used, or not used.

2. Create a process for ongoing sensitivity analysis to market changes.
Operations must have a methodology for constantly recognizing the parameters of its current capabilities. This includes critical supply chain considerations, physical size-volume mix limitations, and other boundaries built into your current operations. An executive initiative that focuses on drawing out this key information—all in the context of sensitivity to market changes—is both responsive and productive.

3. Hold quarterly strategic work sessions for marketing and operations leadership.
Each quarter, marketing and operations leaders should look outside the traditional market view to identify evolving trends and breakthrough performances in other industries. Focusing on being the best at what you currently do is terrific—as long as it doesn't prevent you from taking advantage of moving markets. That's where these quarterly strategic work sessions are incredibly valuable.

Under the guidance of your executive actions, marketing and operations can work together to ensure their strategies align with your strategic vision, and that they're viable for years to come.

STRATEGY #14:

DEVELOP A LONG-RANGE PURPOSE

When I was a corporate employee, we had an annual tradition of creating a five-year strategic plan. Each year, we'd hunker down and pour our efforts into detailing a plan for the next five years. Notably, this process never included an evaluation of the previous year's strategic plan. "Create the new plan; don't worry about the old one!" seemed to be the message from the top. And so we did. No matter how hard we worked on those plans, however, they were always essentially worthless. Why? Because the world changes far too rapidly for even the most brilliant long-range plan to remain relevant and valuable after a year—or even less—has passed.

Fortunately, most companies have realized this by now. They've moved from five-year, to three-year, and on to one-year strategic plans instead. I applaud this shift. Still, many of those organizations continue to undervalue the importance of defining a long-range purpose, beyond just making money for shareholders. They're so caught up in detailing a strategic plan, that they ignore the need for a strategic purpose—one that employees and stakeholders alike can be passionate about.

A meaningful long-range purpose provides context for all decisions in your business. But in order for your long-range purpose to be meaningful, it must first be relevant. That is, relevant to the needs of your customers, the expectations of your stakeholders, and—above all—the lives of your employees.

Without a meaningful long-range purpose, your employees will think: "You want me to work hard to make someone else rich? For no other reason than a paycheck? I don't want to spend my life this way." But with a meaningful long-range purpose, your employees will have a reason to feel passionate about their work and become committed to your organization. These are both essential components to your company's long-term success.

Simply put, long-range planning is a waste of time, but developing a long-range purpose is critically important. By the same token, long-range values and long-term strategic direction are indispensible to achieving consistency, excellence, and long-term success at your company.

Toyota, for example, has focused on the "accident-free vehicle" for decades. Now, facing shifting market demands, they're changing their 25-year view to "safe, environmentally-sound mobility." By the same token, Google started as an internet company, but it's clearly much more than that now. Their mission statement was revamped in 2013 to: "Google's mission is to organize the world's information and make it universally accessible and useful."

When developing your company's long-range purpose, it's important to challenge conventional thinking. After all, you should be focused on what "convention" will look like in a decade or two—not what it looks like today. Every day, the best companies and most successful people challenge conventional thinking, manage risks, and build on their strengths to leverage whatever threats and opportunities emerge from the marketplace.

Much like unproven assumptions, conventional thinking can be a real threat to developing a compelling long-range purpose for your organization. Just consider how conventional thinking contributed to the recent recession, and it's easy to see why.

"Real estate, banking, and utilities are safe investments" was conventional wisdom for almost 70 years. But things changed. People who were living paycheck-to-paycheck with high debt payments—relying on housing inflation and steady income to get them through—contributed mightily to the recession. Homes were repossessed, credit ratings ruined, builders and building supply companies crushed. Financial institutions that facilitated those risky debt levels convulsed, inflicting losses on their investors.

At its core, one could say the recession happened because, for far too long, no one challenged conventional thinking. Don't let the same phenomenon happen to your business. Instead, challenge conventional thinking and be innovative when thinking strategically about your company's long-term purpose in the world.

CHAPTER 3:
ACHIEVING OPERATIONAL EXCELLENCE

"Do not despise the bottom rungs in the ascent to greatness."
—Publilius Syrus

"The lessons learned there fuel the ascent."
—Rebecca Morgan

The majority of small to midsized manufacturing companies don't have an operations strategy. That's right: They flat-out don't have one. As you might imagine, it's incredibly difficult for companies to achieve operational excellence when they don't even have an operations strategy to begin with.

The problem is, most manufacturers think they have an operations strategy, when they actually don't. For decades, manufacturing organizations have relied on the "whatever it takes" mantra to form the basis of their approach to operations. But if you want true operational excellence, that's not a real strategy at all.

This chapter is all about operational excellence—from forming a core operations strategy, to fostering the right operations culture, and achieving critical alignment between marketing and operations. It's a sharp departure from the traditional "get order, fill order" mindset that dominates most manufacturing operations.

If you want operational excellence at your organization, you must remember: Marketing defines brand promise, and operations delivers it—or not. If operations can't deliver the promise that marketing defines for your target customers, then your credibility is shot. Operational excellence is about delivering brand promise every day, all the time, in every single interaction. The following six strategies show you how.

STRATEGY #15:

TRANSFORM YOUR OPERATIONS

Marketing serves a very important role in the manufacturing business. It determines where there's demand, assesses market opportunity, and then goes about creating an "aura" around our products. The Nike swoosh, for example. But as delightful and important as that swoosh is, we still don't want our sneakers to fall apart. And that's where operations steps in.

It's increasingly important that operations understands the brand promise—and delivers it to customers. If customers expect one thing, and then get another, they're more disappointed than if their expectations hadn't been set in the first place. People might like the clever tagline, or the eye-catching logo, but they're going to tell their neighbors about how well—or how poorly—the operations performed.

If you want to transform your business, start by transforming your operations. There's no other way. A new ad campaign can't do it, nor can a new logo. A new vision, mission, and value statement can't do it. The only way to lastingly transform your business into something new and better is to transform your operations. The three aspects of operational transformation are integration, operations strategy, and performance. Mastery of all three is required to revolutionize your operations and your business.

If you want to transform your business, start by transforming your operations. There's no other way."

I'm now going to give you a simple diagnostic tool to use so you can see where you currently are—and how to move forward. It's my trademarked concept, Transforming Operations. Transforming Business. SM Take a look:

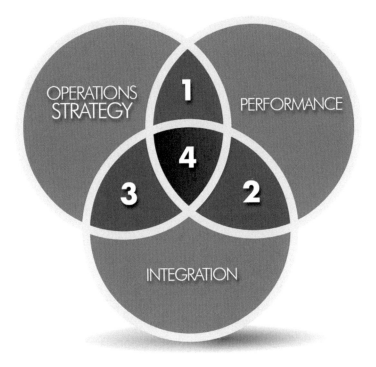

TRANSFORMING OPERATIONS. TRANSFORMING BUSINESS.™

1.Disconnected   2. Reactionary   3. Dreaming   4. Transformational

Using the Venn diagram above, honestly assess how well your company achieves each of these three components: operations strategy, performance, and integration. Grab a pen, and get started.

For each component, place an "X" to indicate whether it's an operational strength for your company. Place the "X" near the central intersection if you believe your company does it well, and place the "X" closer to the outer edge of the circle if you think it's a weakness at your organization.

Take a look at where you placed your three marks. If all three are near the outer edges of the circles, then transforming your business can't happen until you remarkably improve mastery in each of those areas. The processes of converting each facet to a strength can be transformational for your organization, but not for the business itself.

If you consider both your operations strategy and performance to be strengths, but integration is a weakness, then tight integration with marketing and finance is what stands between you and the metamorphosis you seek.

If you consider both performance and integration to be strengths, but your operations strategy is a weakness, then a well-conceived process for the development of a strong operations strategy will propel your desired transformation.

And finally, if you consider your operations strategy and integration to be strengths, but performance is a weakness, then your great intentions are ruined by repeatedly waking to an unsatisfactory reality.

If you consider your operations strategy, performance, and integration all to be great strengths, then you're already capable of transforming your operations and your business. In fact, you're probably already doing it with both speed and effectiveness.

It's still important to continually align these efforts with your mission, vision and, values to ensure that your focus hasn't drifted. Build on your strengths as you eliminate weaknesses that stand in your way.

STRATEGY #16:

RECOGNIZE WHY EXCELLENCE MATTERS

Why does excellence matter? Why should you aim for it at all? These are loaded questions, and they're best answered with a cautionary tale. A few months ago, I received a call from the general manager of the $250 million division of an enormous holding company. He had been with the company for only nine months, but during that time a perfect storm of international conditions had increased orders by 75 percent. Lead times had stretched from a predictable four weeks to over twelve. Quality problems were expanding and employees were exhausted from mandatory six and seven days-per-week production.

Despite all that, profits remained strong. The general manager said he was concerned about purchasing and scheduling, as it wasn't scalable. Scheduling was done by department leads as they printed work orders from the ERP system, and they told people to run them by the oldest due date. Purchasing issued releases against blanket purchase orders, again, per the ERP report. The general manager was also frustrated because he'd been blindsided by a supplier capacity limitation, one that his team had never considered. It was taking months to resolve.

Walking through his operations, we discussed his exasperation further. Then he blew my mind. He said that purchasing and scheduling are really simple and that his people must just not be up to the task. Rather than hire a consultant, he would simply shift scheduling over to purchasing and replace the current staff with more educated people. He declared the processes couldn't be all that bad, since everyone else uses ERP to run their operations, too.

From the way he viewed and handled his problems, it was glaringly apparent that he had no concept of what excellence is, what it takes— or why it matters. He opted to slap Band Aids on a plethora of issues, instead of addressing their root causes, and improving the operations of the division for the long haul.

This is an educated man and I think an ethical one. While his intention to define a problem in very simple terms was a good one, he unfortunately missed the point. He now had responsibility for an area in which he had no expertise. He lacked the confidence to admit he had a lot to learn.

His team did have limited skills, but they weren't the root cause of the problem. I'm sad to say, but not surprised, that months later, his lead time and quality problems continue. Backlog is dropping as customers are choosing other options, but profit margins remain strong so corporate pressures are limited.

Ah, but what could have been. That general manager wasted an incredible opportunity to increase market share, profits and cash, and build processes and capabilities to buttress a $500 million company, all the while demonstrating respect for people and a commitment to excellence.

That's the lynchpin of this story: He didn't have a commitment to excellence. Profits can hide a cornucopia of bad decisions and missed opportunities. And when your only goal is profits—and not excellence—it's sure to happen. That's why, years ago, I realized that I'm not here to help companies who aren't already committed to becoming excellent. I focus my energies on those who are. Life is way too short for mediocrity.

When talking about operational excellence, it's also incredibly important to discuss follow-through. That is, what happens after you implement changes and improvements meant to propel your organization toward excellence. Far too many manufacturers skip the follow-through process, leaving them shipwrecked as they float aimlessly through a sea of half-finished initiatives. I call this "shipwreck excellence"—and it's something you should take great pains to avoid.

There are nine key steps to effectively improving operations on the way to operational excellence:

1. Understand the problem or opportunity
2. Define the goal of making the next change
3. Identify and analyze your options
4. Plan the change that's expected to best accomplish the goal
5. Fully implement the change
6. Follow up to assess the actual impact of the change, versus the expected impact

7 .Learn by examining those differences
8. Verify the change is still in place as designed, and modify procedures as needed
9. Revisit the first step with your new insights

Walking through hundreds of factories over the years, I've observed that the majority of mid-level operations execute some of step three (identifying and analyzing options), some of step four (plan the change) and a little bit of step five (fully implement the change). Then, they simply move on.

Most companies want to be more effective, but they just don't have the committed discipline to do so. I suspect confusion of action and results is at play. But so is a ridiculous waste of time and resources.

The primary distinction between excellent operations and mediocre operations is respect for employees—and their time—and disciplined leadership to execute every one of these steps, for every change made. It might sound slow and boring, but it's actually fast and effective, as your team develops the relevant thinking skills.

Be excellent—not shipwreck excellent. You and your employees will have a much better chance of reaching your destination.

STRATEGY #17:

OPTIMIZE FLOW IN YOUR OPERATIONS

I've looked under the hood of operations at hundreds of manufacturers over the years. In every case, I've seen interruptions to flow somewhere along the line. For many manufacturers, these interruptions go unnoticed—or simply unaddressed—for far too long. Being able to identify and fix interruptions to flow is a skill that can help you reduce costs, lower your investment, and decrease lead-times, all while improving quality. This is true from product development through production and on to post-sale support.

In a perfect manufacturing world, raw materials and components would show up exactly when and where they're needed in production. The item would flow from step to step, with value being added continuously in as little space as possible. When finished, the item would immediately ship to the customer without delay. Nothing would be wasted: not time, not space, not money.

In all my years as a consultant, I've never seen a manufacturer operate that smoothly. I doubt I ever will. But I do work with many companies that strive to come as close as they can to achieving interruption-free flow in their operations.

When it comes to manufacturing operations, progress is made by both creating flow and eliminating interruptions to flow. First, you must be able to see and care about the difference.

Anywhere you see inventory sitting, you see an interruption to flow. Anytime you see product being moved from one place to another, you see non-value added activity—and that's an interruption to flow. Anytime you see a quality inspection or a repair activity, you see an interruption to flow. Anytime you see value important to the customer not being added at that very moment, you're seeing interruption to flow.

Even the best companies in the world don't have continuous flow, but they realize it. They're passionate about improving that condition. They know that "pull systems" like Kanban are an intermediate method of scheduling and inventory control, but they're not the end-goal. They know that warehouses indicate an inability to make what the customer wants, when the customer wants it. Their mantra is: "Flow when you can, pull when you must, and never push."

The details of excellence in operations can vary by industry and market, but optimizing flow will always be an important priority in getting there.

STRATEGY #18:

GAUGE YOUR ORGANIZATION'S SPEED

Every manufacturer knows that speed drives success, yet we all also know that speed kills. If you're changing faster than your organization can handle, it might implode. If you're changing more slowly than you could, valuable progress is forever lost. The trick is to know not only how to accelerate, but how, when, and what to decelerate.

Which activities should you eliminate? Which should you slow? Do you have the right change leaders in place to manage deceleration? It might sound counterintuitive, but frequently there are activities you should accelerate while decelerating others.

Focus on maximizing value to all stakeholders. Make appropriate improvements at the right time and speed to constantly deliver value. Sharp curves appear unannounced. Treacherous peril can emerge from the shadows. Those who recognize the racing line, and know when to brake, when to decelerate, and when to accelerate, will win the race.

The ability to gauge your organization's ideal speed is increasingly important to business success—and to operational excellence. Lead times that were once acceptable will now kill a business. New products with significantly upgraded capabilities are expected at least annually, if not more frequently. Immediate appropriate response to customer concerns is our only hope for preventing social media suicide.

There isn't one aspect of your business that your market doesn't expect to occur more rapidly than it did a year ago. This means that organizational speed is an attribute that must be mastered. But until you've mastered it, it's essential to resist the temptation to move faster than you successfully can.

Butchered orders, invoices, upgrades or new products are each capable of shutting your business down forever. It's not enough to talk speed to employees and suppliers. The only way to master speed is to optimize processes, eliminate bureaucracy, and develop the thinking skills of every employee you have. Methods of reliability testing that require less elapsed time, but are as robust as whatever method you use now, must be developed. Material handling must be efficient and incoming inspections must become a thing of the past.

We all know that time-to-market can have a significant impact on market share and profitability. Have you cut your time-to-market by at least 50 percent in the most recent 3 years? Are you able to cut it by another 50 percent in the next three? If you believe your organization needs to focus on speed, prioritize the areas to attack and look to an expert to help you with the appropriate drills.

Amazingly high-quality risk assessment and management must become integral to everything you do. Organizational understanding of the need for speed in all productive activities is imperative, yet so is the understanding that reckless speed can kill the company. I encourage you to start by identifying and eliminating all non-required non-productive activities. That by itself will accelerate your journey. Let's buckle up.

STRATEGY #19:

LEVERAGE YOUR S&OP PRACTICES

While sales and operations planning methodology has been around for decades, few manufacturers obtain its full potential value. For true operational excellence, you must be one of the rare manufacturers who leverages your sales and operations (S&OP) practices. Let me describe four aspects of this process that are routinely emphasized in companies that leverage it best:

1. A clear and common understanding of what they're trying to accomplish. Organizations who are the

best at S&OP know exactly what they're trying to accomplish through the process. They also know to what degree those needs are currently being satisfied. Seems simple enough: Know what success looks like. Unfortunately, many organizations focus on the task and not on the outcome. Take time to define how you'll know if your company is better off because of its S&OP process. Then consider how well you're currently meeting that potential.

2. Monthly reviews of significant deviations from what's expected. The second S&OP best practice is to execute

monthly reviews of significant deviations from what's expected. Check your results, and learn from them. Then make changes to data, alter your assumptions, and modify the process as appropriate to incorporate your new findings. As you get better at S&OP, your definition of significant deviation will tighten. That's a sign of progress.

3. A three-way conversation between sales, operations, and finance. Effective S&OP isn't a forecast

followed by an MRP-generated production and purchasing plan. Rather, it's a productive conversation between sales, operations, and finance. Operations is responsible for providing feedback to make the sales plan better. Accounting needs to understand the financial risks of planned product introductions and roll-outs, of inventory builds, and of capacity changes. Successful S&OP reflects the inputs of all three teams, and it's then used by all three to move forward.

4. A focus on forecast quality over forecast accuracy. The final S&OP best practice is to focus on forecast quality over forecast accuracy. Forecasts are never accurate, but they can be good enough to enable the leadership team to make high-quality decisions. Think specifically about the types of decisions that are made based on forecast data. Then develop a common understanding of the value in improving the quality of those decisions. To the degree that better forecasting improves decision making, focus on that. If forecast error isn't the cause of poor decisions, focus on what is.

Don't have a monthly S&OP meeting just because you think you should. Instead, develop a process with these four best practices in mind to bring real value to your organization.

STRATEGY #20:

CHAMPION A SAFETY CULTURE

Missing fingers, deaths, severe cuts, and head injuries. Some of the more significant injuries that occur all too often in manufacturing, these horrific experiences result primarily from lack of a safety culture, and the belief of a well-intentioned employee that a shortcut can be done quickly enough to be done safely. The second cause rarely happens when a true culture of safety exists.

Without safety at the heart of your operations strategy, you can't achieve true operational excellence. Meeting Occupational Health and Safety (OSHA) requirements, requiring monthly safety training, and establishing a safety committee are certainly good, but insufficient to create and maintain a culture of safety.

I've seen many operations with above-industry-average safety records, but very few with a true culture of safety. If we pay attention to safety as if every employee is our family member, and constantly reinforce that message at every opportunity, good things seemingly unrelated to safety will happen.

It's impossible to build supremacy in desirable attributes such as trust, focus on operating procedures, and customer service, without the shared experience of a culture of safety. Do more than the minimum. Be your brother's keeper. Consider these five steps to create a culture of safety as you work toward operational excellence:

1. Provide foundational safety education for all employees. Entry-level safety requires compliance with regulatory intent, as well as the letter of the law. OSHA and many factory insurers provide free or very inexpensive education for all your employees. Use it. Failure to support this basic training is dereliction. There are companies who don't grant their employees foundational safety education, but I wouldn't want anyone I care about to work for them. Would you?

2. Provide comprehensive safety education for all employees.

Basic safety education is good; comprehensive safety education is better. Educating employees on all aspects of work-related safety, including ergonomics, can eliminate injuries. Take the time to explain the "why" of all personal protective equipment (PPE) and never make exceptions to it. Too often, I see construction workers performing jobs like sawing wood or cement without protective eyewear. If management at your company allows that kind of irresponsible behavior, find new management. Responsible management that cares about employees wouldn't let that happen. It would say: "Wear your PPE, or find another job."

3. Make safety a personal responsibility.

Safety is a choice. Management can provide all the education and protective equipment in the world—but an employee committed to violating safety rules will do so. No employee wants to get hurt, but many believe they can do something safely without adhering to safety rules. Every individual makes the decision to be safe or not. Ensure anyone seen acting in an unsafe manner is taken aside, coached, and not allowed to continue that way. Don't let anyone think you care so little about them that you would let them behave unsafely. That includes office personnel and visitors walking through controlled areas. Anyone repeatedly choosing to be unsafe is choosing a different place to work.

❝

Without safety at the heart of your operations strategy, you can't achieve true operational excellence."

4. Problem solve safety issues. Many companies use A3
or 8D or the 5 Why's to understand and solve production problems. But too few use those same root-cause rigorous problem-solving techniques to prevent future accidents. When accidents or near-misses occur, treat them with a disciplined approach. Instead of saying, "The employee was careless!" find out why. Were the gloves or eye protection too far away, so the employee didn't want to take the time to go get them? You can easily fix that by providing PPE supplies at points of use. Take the time to identify root causes and countermeasures that prevent reoccurrence.

Filing government reports is insufficient. Put as much brainpower into problem solving safety issues as you put into quality or productivity challenges. And don't wait for someone to get hurt. Use that same thinking to identify potential injury situations and change them.

5. Extend the reach of safety beyond your
gates. Safety doesn't end at the gates to your manufacturing plant. I've visited manufacturing plants in one of Mexico's most dangerous cities. Management there puts as much emphasis on safety outside the facility as in it. Instead of worrying about nickels and dimes, one manufacturer I know encourages team members to take eye protection home to use when mowing the lawn. Another provides a high-quality car seat to every new baby born to an employee.

Your coworkers may face health concerns from poor diet, stress, and lack of exercise. You can help them return to work as healthy as they left it through positive lifestyle training and incentives. Is it your job? I don't know. But how much do you care about your employees? If workers are expected to go "above and beyond," then leadership should, too.

Accidents might still happen, but an excellent company moves beyond policies and rules to create a culture of safety. It's important to show true caring by preventing potentially dangerous behaviors. Who are you willing to see get hurt today? If the answer is no one, then create a culture that demonstrates that—and tell every employee nothing else is acceptable.

CHAPTER 4:
GETTING LEAN, THE RIGHT WAY

"It's not so important who starts the game but who finishes it."
—John Wooden

"For a win, the game must be finished. Starting things without
finishing them is quitting, and no great team does that."
—Rebecca Morgan

Many people believe that lean manufacturing is the only way to be operationally excellent. While this isn't necessarily true, lean manufacturing is extremely common at high-performing manufacturers. And, when the philosophy is fully integrated, lean can transform an average company into a great one.

Unfortunately, many manufacturers don't truly understand what lean is. They implement "lean strategies" in a haphazard way, never taking the time to understand what lean actually is. Other companies put effective lean tools into place, but fail to implement a lean management system. Without a clear understanding of lean manufacturing, and a high-level lean management system in place, any attempt at lean will soon erode. I see it all the time: Companies make great strides with lean, but then they inevitably slide backward. There's no strategy in place to make things stick, or to manage the lean efforts going on in the factory.

Getting lean the "right way" is about making sure that lean becomes deeply ingrained in your organization. If you don't, you'll go back to business as usual as soon as the first crisis arises.

The following five strategies provide key insights into becoming lean in a way that will stay with your organization for continued operational success.

STRATEGY #21:

AIM FOR LEAN, IN ITS TRUEST FORM

Lean manufacturing is a term that's maligned, denounced, discredited, and disparaged. It's also extolled, celebrated, advocated, and praised. How can one term provoke such passionate controversy? Well, people's penchant for finding a silver bullet undermines their ability to see the system behind the tools. As a result, lean manufacturing is often misunderstood and misrepresented.

Before you can begin to "go lean" at your organization, it's crucial that you first understand what lean is, in its truest form. Let me make this perfectly clear: Lean manufacturing is a thinking system that includes tools; it's not a system of tools. Importantly, these tools were developed to solve specific problems that Toyota had at very specific times, in specific parts of their operations. This means that the tools included in lean manufacturing may or may not help you. And if they do, they'll likely require modification from what Toyota originally designed. After all, your operations are different from theirs—and so are your problems.

The word "lean" is actually an Americanized label selected by a book editor to summarize the Toyota Production System—and systems similar to it—practiced by other Japanese companies decades ago. Lean manufacturing, in its truest form, is then a generic term for the production and business systems used by successful Japanese companies after World War II.

Desperate times call for desperate actions, and after World War II many Japanese manufacturers were very desperate. They began questioning how everything was currently being done. They reduced change-over times so they could produce smaller batches, which would then allow them to reduce lead times and inventory investment. They found that the immediate feedback that small batches enabled was also valuable in improving quality. They also recognized that they were doing work that wasn't important to their customers, so they figured out how to quit doing it. They began to develop Voice of the Customer (VOC) processes to ensure they had current understanding of customer wants and expectations.

They knew that every worker had to contribute to their success, as they couldn't afford to live with problems or wait for management to get smart enough to solve them. They invested in their workers, and partnered with their suppliers so they could all not only survive, but thrive.

The only thing "Japanese" about "lean" is that Japan is where the commitment to getting better every day, focusing on the customer, developing all employees as problem solvers, showing true respect for people, and eliminating waste was first codified as a coherent production and business philosophy. When you understand that description of lean, you quickly see that it can be valuable to every business. These are hardly quirky concepts, but many manufacturers have been unable or unwilling to incorporate them deeply within the essence of their company.

To some people, lean means eliminating people. To others, it only applies in industries like car manufacturing. To still others, it's something they tried and concluded doesn't work for them. And sadly for yet others, it means yellow lines painted on the floor, and 5S trophies moved from one department to the next each month. The Toyota Production System, commonly considered the same as lean manufacturing in North America, is a fully integrated system of managerial, philosophical, and technical pillars all devoted to the development of people.

Any company that describes its operations as lean but doesn't have the development of people as its focus is doing something other than what Toyota is talking about.

In short, just because companies call their operations lean, doesn't mean they are. This doesn't make them wrong. It just means that whatever efforts they're making aren't based on Toyota's successful system. If you've decided that lean manufacturing is right for your business, then aim for lean in its truest form.

Lean manufacturing is a thinking system that includes tools; it's not a system of tools."

STRATEGY #22:

UNDERSTAND WHY LEAN FAILS

When something fails over 90 percent of the time, it's usually tossed to the curb. Lean implementations fail at least that often: Over 75 percent of organizations that try lean give up in under 24 months. Another 20 percent keep stumbling along, never realizing the potential of lean. Why does lean fail so often—and why do companies keep trying?

The "keep trying" part is easy. There are countless stories of great results from lean, so it's no wonder why companies continue to attempt lean transformation. And lean is often the answer to organizations' widespread desperation to try anything to become more competitive in manufacturing.

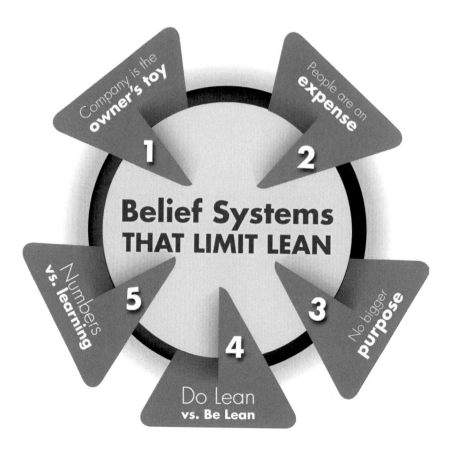

In the vast majority of cases where lean fails, organizations almost implement lean, but don't get it quite right. Don't be one of those organizations. Before you can implement lean, you must understand the five most common beliefs that cause lean to fail:

1. Company is the owner's toy. One of the most common factors limiting lean success is the philosophical wall of "the company is the owner's asset." This perception limits the commitment of every other stakeholder. Common symptoms of this include any change in leadership leading to a change in business operating philosophy, or the owner not understanding or participating in lean behaviors.

2. People are an expense. When people are viewed as an expense, there will always be trouble. The belief that people are an expense is frequently reflected in layoffs, and reductions in training and development during slow times. None of that is conducive to successful lean implementation.

3. No bigger purpose. If a company has no bigger purpose than to make money there is little chance that all stakeholders will throw their full effort into making the company better. Developing employees is clearly a secondary, or less, issue in this kind of organization.

4. Do lean vs. Be lean. When leadership says "we want to do lean" instead of "we want to become lean" it rarely understands the pervasive nature of organizational change required. This simple issue of semantics can usually signal whether a company will be successful with lean, or not.

5. Numbers vs. learning. When the numbers are more important than learning, the organization won't be able to implement lean successfully. Management must give just as much weight to what's been learned as it does to numbers on a chart. Learning drives performance improvements.

This brings us to one of the most common sources of lean failure: management. Take a look at the five most pervasive management causes of failed lean implementations:

MANAGEMENT CAUSES OF LEAN FAILURE

1. Unchanged management system. Lean is unlikely to fit well into current management systems, yet management rarely thinks its processes need to change. The managers that fail to understand that management systems must change are the same ones who express frustration at repeat problems. Band-Aids make a simple system complex and fail to drive problems from the business.

2. Failure to see the whole. Companies tend to focus on how instead of why, who, and when. It's easy to hire a trainer to educate employees on lean tools, and then insist that they begin to implement those tools. But that alone will never be sustained. For example, most companies begin with the tool known as 5S. They make quick, visible progress with the first three S's—sort, set in order, and shine—but they struggle mightily with the fourth and fifth—standardize and sustain. Then the first three S's slide into history, leaving useless stripes on the floor and unused shadow boards as evidence.

Standardize and sustain are aspects of lean, both tools and philosophy, that stymie most companies. To master these two S's, you must learn to integrate the why, the who, and the when into your lean transformation—not just the how.

3. Focus on blame. When there's a culture of blame instead of a focus on improving process, lean is absent. Additionally, problem solving can require new skills and time that some managers just aren't willing to give. Rather, they're content to assign blame to employees for problems, without ever addressing root cause.

4. Results vs. Process. Lean is a thinking system that includes tools, not a system of tools. When leadership doesn't understand this basic fact, there's a low ceiling on improvement. Slapping tools on a factory without specific just-in-time purpose that matters to employees, and on top of whatever is already in place, won't work. Yet, it's a common form of "lean implementation." That effort is typically led by someone who fails to realize that Toyota designed tools to meet its needs, not anyone else's, and that tools are a means to an end and not an end in themselves.

Copy-paste isn't a good approach, especially when you don't understand what you're copying.

5. Standard cost accounting. Most manufacturing companies use a standard cost accounting system. There's no better way to stop your lean journey dead in its tracks. Standard cost accounting is the root of all evil in terms of trying to improve your organization. That's because it was developed when big batches were the norm, and it's focused on expensive change overs. What's more, standard cost accounting uses inscrutable language and leads to bad business decisions, like absorbing overhead by building more product than you actually need.

So why does lean fail so often? Because it's not nearly as simple as it seems. Successful lean implementations require significant and pervasive change throughout most organizations—with constant reinforcement of the behavioral adjustments. It's not a silver bullet, nor is it quick. Like weight control and smoking cessation, people start with good intentions. Some make immediate and noticeable changes. But it's much more difficult to make the changes stick for life.

I encourage you to look at every mistake and failure on your path to becoming lean as an opportunity to learn and grow. Slow progress is still progress. It's only failure if you quit learning.

STRATEGY #23:

DON'T CUT COSTS TO CUT CORNERS

Most manufacturers are focused entirely on reducing cost—often to the exclusion of things that are much more important. The reality is, you can't cut your way to the top, especially when it comes to lean. While many executives think "lean" is synonymous with "cutting costs," that couldn't be further from the truth.

Reductions in cost are really a result of improving other capabilities. Some people think they can reduce costs with lean manufacturing. In fact, if you understand what lean is, you'll end up with lower costs—but that's not what lean is about. Your reductions in cost are a result of improving other aspects of your organization.

For example, if you increase your inventory turns, you'll have less risk of obsolescence and mistakes. You'll have less cash tied up and you'll require less space. While it might seem counterintuitive, increasing your inventory turns also improves flexibility and customer service. It's about having the right items, not the most items. Increasing inventory turns also requires less handling so there are fewer opportunities for further bad things to happen. And yes, by the way, increasing inventory turns reduces costs, too.

//
Reductions in cost are really a result of improving other capabilities."

Another example is reducing the movement of product and people. This will save a lot of time, since people won't have to look around for resources. It's a lot faster to give them what they need, where they are, when they need it. Reducing that movement reduces injury opportunities and decreases the chance of damaging product. It also improves productivity. And yes, by the way, it reduces costs, too.

The challenge for many manufacturers is that cost reduction is expected to point to a specific line on the P&L. That's why direct labor savings is such an attractive target. It's right there. It's in a line we can point to. But if you want to lay people off, then do it. You don't need outside help for that.

If, instead, you want to grow the capacity of your existing people and equipment resources to support profitable growth, then lean is an approach that can help you succeed. And yes, by the way, it will reduce costs, too.

STRATEGY #24:

COMMIT TO LEAN MANAGEMENT

Many companies have tried to become lean, failed, and then concluded that "lean doesn't work for them." That's interesting, given that lean includes some fairly simple concepts that should apply to everyone: Focus on the customer, eliminate waste, and develop problem-solving skills in all employees. These concepts really are generally applicable, but they still fail at a lot of organizations.

The primary tactical reason why they fail is that companies don't put a lean management system in place. Companies often have difficulty maintaining the initial gains of lean activities because they keep managing the same old way. That simply doesn't work when you're expecting everyone else to toss out their old behaviors and keep new ones.

LEAN MANAGEMENT SYSTEM

1. Inconsistent   2. Blind   3. Slow   4. Effective

Manufacturers tend to think of lean as being all about changing the operators, changing the lower level people's behavior. We give them standard work, but we don't give ourselves standard work. We hold them accountable, but we don't hold ourselves accountable. So, if you want lean to be integral to your journey of becoming operationally excellent, then you must implement a lean management system. That system has three components:

1. Visual control systems. Visual control systems provide means to quickly detect gaps between "what should be happening" and "what is happening" so that action can be taken to solve the problem. These systems should be implemented throughout your operations including the management and office business arenas. It needs to be obvious when there's a gap between expectation and reality. Those gaps indicate problems or variants from goals, and they deserve attention right away.

2. Daily accountability. The second component of lean management is daily accountability. We can't identify gaps, and then only follow up on them weekly, monthly, or quarterly. There must be daily accountability. Implement a series of daily tiered meetings that encourage employee groups to solve the problems they can—and to quickly raise awareness of those they can't. And then follow up daily on commitments made to ensure follow through.

3. Leader standard work. The third element of a lean management system is leader standard work. A lot of executives think this can't possibly apply to them, because they're leaders and there's no way to have standard work for their jobs. But there is not only a way; there's a need. Leader standard work is the methodology that reinforces the lean execution system and the priorities and commitments made within it. Leader standard work will not define 40 hours of your week as it does for some of your hourly operators. It may only define five to fifteen percent of your week. But that's a very important part of your leadership responsibility in becoming a lean organization that cannot be delegated or forgotten.

These three interwoven elements of lean management might sound easy—and they are, with proper understanding and practice. However, many managers and leaders find them to be just too much change for themselves. As a result, they shrug off the need for lean management, only to find that lean will soon begin to erode. Without methods of detecting gaps and addressing them quickly and reliably, it's obvious why employees drift from new lean behaviors back to their old, non-lean ones.

All three of these elements—visual control systems, daily accountability, and leader standard work—together form a "plan, do, check, adjust" for your lean system. Start with visual controls. Quickly follow up with daily accountability, and then bring in leader standard work. Take a look in the mirror and see what you're doing to make sure that your lean systems are, in fact, leading you to excellence.

STRATEGY #25:

OVERCOME YOUR TECHNICAL LIMITS

The top five percent of manufacturing organizations transitioning to a lean environment successfully address all three arenas of lean manufacturing: technical, managerial, and philosophical. The 75 percent of organizations that quit lean never get very far into the technical arena—and they're largely unaware of the managerial and philosophical aspects. The 20 percent in the middle never really master the technical and managerial facets. Let's make sure your organization gets over that first hump: the technical side of lean.

First off, every tool in lean is designed to solve a problem. None of them will be effective if implemented without a specific purpose, and none will be effective if the approach is copy-pasted from some other company. Use an appropriate lean tool to solve a specific problem that employees care about.

Let's use the lean methodology of 5S as an example. If employees are complaining about a lack of tools, it's a great time to teach the basic concepts of 5S and then immediately go to the floor and start implementing. We all know that your employees aren't thieves. They simply can't find the tool they need, when they need it. In an effort to do their job, they grab the first tool they can find and then hide it so they'll have it next time. Logical behavior of someone who wants to do his job.

In the 5S process, you might find you don't have enough tools. That's a problem you need to solve. It's much more likely that you'll find you have too many of some tools and not enough of others. This is also a great time to incorporate ergonomic education. Locating items so that they are where they are needed—and that no backs are harmed in the performing of this work—improves safety and shows employees that you care.

Most people consider 5S an entry-level lean tool for the shop floor. They can tell you what each of the five S's is and too often suggest that the bottom line is "a place for everything and everything in its place." They lay down yellow tape to outline where the trash can goes, create shadow boards for tools, and issue monthly trophies. None of that is inherently bad, but the concept behind 5S is so much more than that.

When leveraged well, lean tools such as 5S will eliminate waste. Costly clutter exists far beyond the shop floor; in fact, it exists in every aspect of even the best organizations. And as you overcome your technical limits and implement lean tools, you'll steadily remove that clutter.

Have you 5S'd your customer base? What about your products, and the components that go into your products? Over time, those things get just as cluttered as the shop floor, and they can certainly benefit from 5S thinking as well.

Just as some people hang on to tools that haven't been used in years, so too do many companies hang on to customers that simply don't make sense for the business any longer. Get rid of them. They sap valuable resources better used elsewhere.

The same is true for product offerings. It takes resources to support products that long ago lost their market luster. Additionally, too many choices can make it hard for your customers to find just what they're looking for.

One of my clients had over 50 different switches in use to accomplish the same function in very similar products. They've now reduced that to fewer than 10, and haven't given up on eliminating still more switches. Modular design can improve this problems immensely, but so can applying 5S thinking to your existing designs and part numbers.

Some of your suppliers are partners, focused on mutual benefit with you. A quick look at your supplier lists will undoubtedly reveal companies you shouldn't be doing business with any longer. They can't help you succeed and aren't interested in your help in improving their capabilities. Why are they still on your list?

And just as on the shop floor, 5S thinking for your business has to become a way of being—not an annual event.

5S is a thought process designed to resolve a type of problem that occurs throughout your business. I challenge you to apply that seemingly simple tool accordingly. You'll be surprised by all the costly clutter that you can eliminate. As you can see from this single exploration of one lean methodology, it's powerful to implement the technical side of lean well. And once you do, the benefits are far-reaching and powerful. But most companies fail to do so because they can't let go of old ways.

Lean is a transformation, not a toe-in-the-water exercise. When an organization makes the very serious decision to become lean, that means changes in almost every activity currently performed. Letting go of how we've always done things isn't easy. Unexpected problems will arise during the implementation of new methods. Every manager and employee has no choice other than to let go of the old ways and improve the new ways. Using tools to resolve problems that matter will propel your transformation forward.

CHAPTER 5:
MASTERING SUPPLY CHAIN

"He that is good for making excuses is seldom good for
anything else."
—Benjamin Franklin

"Excuses can identify problems that need to be solved.
Take them away."
—Rebecca Morgan

Successful manufacturing is the artful choreography of bringing in the right materials at the right time, to create products for customers who need them and want them. The next routine of the dance is getting those products to the customers—exactly when they need them and want them.

From your suppliers' suppliers, to your customers' customers, it's all about getting things into the right hands, at exactly the right time. It should come as no surprise that your manufacturing business can't be excellence without excellent supply chain management. Your internal operations might be exceptional. But what good does that do if your distribution can't get products to your customers?

Far too many people believe that manufacturing is separate from the supply chain. It's not. Manufacturing is part of the supply chain. Manufacturing companies simply choose to manufacture certain aspects of the supply chain. You could buy what you make from somebody else—you just decide to produce it instead.

You're not in the business of making things; you're in the business of supplying something of value to your customers. Make sure you supply it well, and on time. A manufacturing company without a successful supply chain is nothing. The following six strategies shed light on how to master this critical aspect of your business.

STRATEGY #26:

FOCUS ON PROFITABLE GROWTH

There was a time when supply chain teams were only expected to focus on negotiating the lowest purchase price. Not so anymore. The best manufacturing organizations have moved far beyond a simple focus on reducing costs. In fact, the strongest supply chain teams can adroitly manage costs while managing risks—all with a laser-focus on creating opportunities for profitable growth.

In manufacturing, supply chain risks include such varied elements as supplier stability and capacity, material and technology changes, and many ever-popular government and industry regulations. These are all key sources of risks that your supply chain team should be managing. At the same time, your company should also be looking to increase revenues as a direct result of effective supply chain management.

How? The basics are two-fold: 100 percent on-time delivery to customer expectations, and zero deviations—in the product, the invoice, and all aspects of the customer relationship. But equally important is developing suppliers who contribute a competitive advantage to your organization.

To better explain the key priorities that must work together for a supply-chain focus on profitable growth, I've created the diagram below:

SUPPLY CHAIN MANAGEMENT & PROFITABLE GROWTH

1. Stagnant   2. Expensive   3. House of Cards   **4. Profitable Growth**

As you can see, true profitable growth lives at the intersection of managing costs, managing risks, and supporting revenue, all with equal success. If your supply chain team focuses on managing both costs and risks, but fails to pursue actions that support revenue, then the result is stagnancy.

If, on the other hand, your supply chain team is focused on managing risks and supporting revenue, but doesn't focus on managing costs, then you're choosing an expensive strategy. Believe it or not, some high-margin companies make this choice on purpose—but for most organizations, it's a money pit.

Now, let's say your supply chain team focuses on managing costs and supporting revenue, but ignores risk management. In this case, you're living in a house of cards. When you least expect it, Murphy's Law will strike—and you'll be wholly unprepared for it. As you begin to reassess and strengthen your existing supply chain strategy, keep this diagram at the forefront. Make sure your entire supply chain team understands that a balance among these three responsibilities—managing risks, managing costs, and supporting revenue—is the only way to manage a supply chain to create profitable growth for the company.

STRATEGY #27:

EXPERTLY MANAGE THE RISK OF CRITICAL MASS

North Carolina had its textile industry. Detroit had its cars. Silicon Valley is currently the home of high-tech in the United States, replacing Massachusetts' Highway 128. Electronics are concentrated in Southeast Asia. And, of course, there was the offshoring of a multitude of high-labor-content components to low-wage countries that created similar economic enclaves there.

That critical mass made recruiting trained people and locating local experienced sources and all the support and connecting industries much easier. Great things happened. However, in several of those cases, the critical mass subsequently resulted in major negative economic impact to companies, communities, and people. Mayhem, some might call it.

If your business is in a location that depends on critical mass for specialized suppliers and talent, be both appreciative and aware. For example, if key employees merely rotate within competitive companies in the same area, the recruiting benefits of critical mass have been reversed.

If your suppliers are located in such an enclave, or in politically charged geographies, backup plans are an important part of your risk management. For example, back in 2014, Hong Kong, a great and stable financial capital for decades, had over 100,000 protesters in the streets, with police using tear gas. Around the same time, Russia's supply of gas to Europe was threatened, and New York City saw over 100,000 march in support of action to limit and reverse global warming. Not long after, Vietnamese workers set fire to factories owned or managed by the Chinese as a reaction to perceived political provocations.

All of this only a few short years after tsunamis and earthquakes in Japan destroyed power sources, infrastructure, and businesses. Likewise, if all your electronics come from the Philippines, remember that country is regularly exposed to major destructive cyclones.

The examples above show how critical mass that initially provides benefit will heighten risk when taken too far. Increasing unrest, intensifying weather patterns, and changing geopolitical relationships or industry restructuring can turn the gains of critical mass into the loss of economic viability.

Critical mass must be expertly managed to avoid this pitfall.

STRATEGY #28:

DEVELOP AN INVENTORY STRATEGY

I recently worked with a client to develop an inventory strategy. In this particular business, at that particular time, it made sense to focus on a finished goods strategy first. The inventory analyst drafted that strategy and then reviewed it with me. Unfortunately, the strategy he showed me was an Excel spreadsheet. It had a row for every SKU, or stock keeping unit, and it had a cost number and a target inventory number. When I asked him to explain the strategy that led to those numbers, I got a very blank stare. He believed those numbers were the strategy.

This was certainly not the first company, nor the first inventory analyst, I've worked with who didn't understand what an inventory strategy really is. There are many elements that go into developing an effective inventory strategy. Here are three key considerations that will help you develop a strong inventory strategy, turning your inventory into useful cash instead of wasted money:

1. The strategy defines the rule. Understand that, as conditions change, your target quantities may change to stay within the rules or guidelines of your strategy. Now, the inventory analyst I mentioned above told me that one of his target levels was two to three weeks of average sales. I challenged him to think deeper about whether that was a good target. We talked about variation in demand, about manufacturing lead times, about supply issues of materials and components that went into that part, about storage space and handling considerations. The more we talked, the more the light went on for him.

We then created a simple daily exception report that showed him any variations within a rules-based plus or minus of actual target levels. We looked at it daily to learn more about the issues that could impact the rules defined by the strategy. For example, we determined rules for how to identify a probable forecast problem, rather than just blindly changing the inventory target levels. Within a few weeks, he had documented the rules and created easy methods to incorporate those calculations in real time. The thinking, the rules, and the guidelines used to calculate a quantity—those define the strategy. The numbers themselves?

They're just a result of how the strategy incorporates current business conditions.

2. Physical inventory is a waste. Taking a physical inventory wastes more capacity for no benefit than just about any other single operational activity. So why do companies still do it? Statement of inventory value provides one of the easiest ways to impact earnings (ergo, taxes) and balance sheet results. For that reason, auditing firms won't sign off on the financials without some verification of inventories.

Everyone in operations knows that the process of "Stop the presses! We're going to count!" is a wasteful one that changes numbers without improving them. But somehow, this show of massive force convinces the auditors that the numbers are more valid than they were before. Stop the madness! An effective cycle count process—one that identifies and actually fixes problems causing inventory inaccuracies, rather than simply changing quantities in the computer—will eliminate physical inventory within a few short years.

Keep in mind that the traditional "count A items monthly; B items quarterly and C items annually" method is insufficient if you want to eliminate physical inventory. An effective cycle counting process delivers valuable information in a timeframe that facilitates fact–based research and root-cause problem solving. Quit making excuses. You don't have to do a physical inventory. You just need accurate inventories.

3. Surplus inventory can be turned into cash. In the consumer industry, I've had clients with finished goods that were produced to support a forecast that never happened. One way to eliminate that inventory, once you already have it, is to make minor modifications to it and turn it into a product that is currently selling. But you only want to do that if the labor pays for itself.

When you have work-in-process, stop early-stage production until the WIP is reduced to appropriate levels. I know this runs against the grain of the mainstream manufacturing mantra "if you don't start it, you'll never finish it." But if you've got excess WIP, you need to work it off—and therefore not start early-stage production. That will reduce the need for cash and it'll create finished goods that you can then sell. Of course, it's best not to create surplus inventory in the first place.

My best clients have learned how to increase turns, cash, and service levels at the same time. These three considerations in developing a strong inventory strategy will help you establish a successful approach to your inventory, so you can do the same.

STRATEGY #29:

LIMIT SUPPLY CHAIN EXPOSURE

It's common knowledge that supply chains have inherent risk. Most manufacturers have a healthy fear of "acts of nature," major labor strikes or lockouts, and "world-wide shortage" interruptions. It's easy for manufacturing executives to give far more credence to these Big Bang potential risks than to the daily internal high-risk behaviors of their own organizations. While all are important, consider these three specific examples of daily practices impacting exposure that you may have overlooked:

1. Email communication with suppliers: Everyone
knows that email isn't a secured form of communication, yet companies continue to transmit confidential information that way with regularity. As a general rule, if you wouldn't email something to your competitors, don't email it to your suppliers. We laugh at the "don't use this information inappropriately" paragraphs at the bottom of emails from attorneys, yet send confidential information via email regularly. Consider putting in place secured supplier and customer portals. Make sure your organization and your suppliers use these portals exclusively when communicating confidential information. While few things are truly effectively secret, there's no reason to carelessly spread what you intended to keep unpublished.

2. Supplier treatment of your confidential
information: Even with a secured portal in place for
communication with your suppliers, the question of what they then do with the information remains. How can you be sure that they treat the information as carefully as you expect? The answer is "trust, but verify." Suppliers have employees, other customers, and their own suppliers. And each of those groups may not appreciate confidentiality as it impacts your organization. Examine the systems you have in place to manage your customers' confidential data—and compare them to the information protection processes your suppliers execute. Much of your data is less valuable than you think but a significant amount of it floating around the internet is much too valuable to treat lightly.

3. Suppliers as banks: Far too many CFOs think it's an advantage to pay suppliers more slowly. But how does that make you a more desirable customer? It doesn't. Paying suppliers slowly reduces their incentive to improve and become a better partner with your organization. Because of this, treating your suppliers as banks actually puts your supply chain at higher risk.

Supply chain exposure permeates business relationships, and most businesses get hit by a major interruption at some point. A formal risk identification, assessment, and management process should be in place to address those. These three simple daily practices you can manage to limit your supply chain exposure might sound boring—but you never want the excitement of basic errors to jeopardize your supply chain success.

Supply chain exposure permeates business relationships"

STRATEGY #30:

OUTSOURCE WITH CARE

You can outsource activity, but you can't outsource responsibility. To ensure a strong supply chain, you must outsource with this in mind. Outsourcing is more than just managing purchase orders. It requires communication, problem solving, and the ability to integrate with systems and processes other than your own.

Outsourcing can be a good strategy. But too many people think that once they issue purchase orders, they're done. Not so. Outsourcing must be a well-developed, tight, well-communicated relationship with other companies. In fact, the best outsourcing relationships don't act like a bunch of independent companies tied together with purchase orders. Instead, they behave as interconnected companies that happen to have different owners.

To take a further look at outsourcing, let's turn to two of the biggest companies out there: Boeing and Apple. Boeing is perceived as old, plodding, and bureaucratic, while Apple is perceived as young, cutting edge, and agile. Both have stumbled mightily in their outsourcing activities.

In 2014, the Boeing Dreamliner 787 began its first long-awaited commercial flight in the United States. The plane incorporates new technologies and materials, and also represents the shifting of Boeing from a manufacturer to a design and assembly firm. What ensued was a confusion among suppliers, multiple delays, and mid-process redesign of many manufacturing and assembly processes. All make a pretty clear case that successful outsourcing requires a heck of a lot more than issuing purchase orders. Project management, communication, coordination, and even design skills much greater than Boeing could demonstrate were required.

Turning to Apple, lines form as faithful customers can't wait to purchase the next i-Device. However, the outsourced manufacturing and assembly challenges of Apple—best known through the multiple suicides at its Chinese subcontractor Foxconn—received massive publicity in the United States.

For Boeing, the delays meant lost millions, if not billions, of dollars resulting from the incompetence of their Dreamliner outsourcing efforts. But if the plane operates as efficiently as promised, the already significant backlog will likely increase further. For Apple, except for some temporary bad publicity, the behavior of one of its primary subcontractors left it relatively unscathed, with no real harm to sales or profits.

Unless you have their bank accounts—and either Boeing's barriers to entry or Apple's fanatical customer base—your company would not likely be so lucky. Learn from the experiences of both as you outsource key aspects of your business.

//
You can outsource activity, but you can't outsource responsibility."

STRATEGY #31:

TEST AND STRENGTHEN YOUR SUPPLY CHAIN

Emanating from the 2008 bank crisis is legislation that banks deemed too big to fail must undergo a financial stress test. The purpose is to recognize and limit risk to the overall economy. You can modify that concept to recognize and limit the risk to your business and supply chain.

Risk comes in many forms: financial, product failure, and scarcity of key resources are just a few that you may want to prepare for. Identify and prioritize those risks—and then develop a stress test for your supply chain.

Consider your key suppliers and their suppliers. Could they continue to operate and meet your needs if, for example, they experienced a 25 to 50 percent drop in sales? Or if one of their major customers went bankrupt without paying them? Or if energy or other commodity prices skyrocketed? Consider what unexpected political upheavals might threaten your supply chain. Verify that their equipment is well-maintained. And ensure that strategic redundant tooling and outsource capabilities are ready to support your needs.

Whether the stress test you develop includes objective metrics or subjective evaluations, it will help you understand the risks you face. Start with any sole-source suppliers, followed shortly thereafter by suppliers of key materials or components. Develop an evaluation tool that's consistent within a category of suppliers, if not across all of them. Then share it with your supply chain and use it together to manage and minimize risk. Don't wait for a crisis to happen before you begin to prevent one.

Stress testing your supply chain is the critical first step to strengthening your supply chain. And strengthening your supply chain can ensure long-term benefits. Cost management is one place to start—but cost management is in no way synonymous with lowest price. If your team is still beating up suppliers and moving to save a penny, you've missed the point.

The concept of total cost of ownership (TCO) has been around for years, and should be understood by both management and your supply chain personnel. Price, inventory, manufacturing uptime, and lead times are four TCO components that must be understood to truly manage costs. When you've got that one mastered, move along to reducing total supply chain cost, which is where real cost management creates success.

Local optimization doesn't create global optimization, so it's critical for companies to look at handoffs and cross-company processes to ensure the entire chain in both directions is becoming more competitive.

As you work internally to improve your competitive capabilities, look to your suppliers and customers to help you become better. If they don't bring competitive advantage, are they the right partners for you? If they are the right partners, but don't improve your competitive position, what can you do to help them become stronger? Your partners should reduce your time to market, and provide expertise to improve your designs. You should also do the same for them.

If you and your supply chain aren't improving together, you're declining together. Don't let your supply chain bring you down because you were only looking at the weight of your own link.

CHAPTER 6:
PROBLEM SOLVING AND IMPROVING

"Simplicity is the ultimate sophistication."
—Leonardo DaVinci

"Anyone can develop complex solutions,
but the wise insist on finding simplicity."
—Rebecca Morgan

Problems happen all the time in manufacturing. What's critical is how companies choose to deal with those problems. If your employees come to work and experience the same problems every day, they'll get frustrated. If they routinely can't find the tools and materials they need, or they can't work with the designs created by engineering, they'll soon start to feel hopeless. As the leader of your company, it's your job to develop culture and processes to prevent and solve problems.

The foundation of a problem-solving culture is a leader who listens to employees—and then puts the resources in place to allow them to solve their problems. Unfortunately, only a small percentage of manufacturers actually have a problem-solving culture. The vast majority simply say "that's just the way it is" when they see a problem. This dangerous mentality leads to hopelessness in employees, and loss of competitive advantage from resultant poor performance and costs.

But the best manufacturers constantly solve problems. It's a continuous mindset of refusing to accept things the way they are today—and working together to make things better for leadership, employees, investors, communities, and suppliers.

In this chapter, you'll learn five strategies to help you create a problem-solving culture at your organization. The truth is, your company won't survive without one.

STRATEGY #32:

UNDERSTAND YOUR PROBLEMS

The first step of effective problem solving is always to recognize and then understand the problem. Then, and only then, do solutions become relevant. Yet when executives brainstorm the potential root causes of problems, they frequently talk about making changes more than anything else. Why? Because it's easier to make assumptions about what the problem might be—and announce a possible change—than it is to articulate the assumptions inherent in that option.

In asking about the potential root causes of inconsistent product quality, a common answer is, "Change suppliers." Huh? That's not a cause—it's a solution. The idea of "change suppliers" is based on the potential of a current supplier in some way contributing to the inconsistent quality. But how? What conditions would make changing suppliers the right action to drive the problem from the business? Well, that's a bit harder to think about, and much more difficult to articulate.

This type of reasoning—or understanding—is a critical part of the problem-solving process. The inability to describe the reasoning behind an idea limits learning, and limits success. A manufacturer that can drive repeat problems from its business forever will have an incredible advantage over its competition, but to do so requires excellent reasoning skills. Most companies skip understanding the problem and go straight to discussing potential solutions. What a waste of time and resources that is.

If we don't agree on the problem, we'll never agree on the solution. If we make changes without understanding the problem, how will we understand their impact? Change for change's sake is dangerous. It's frustrating to your employees and it doesn't give you the opportunity to learn.

There are several widely used problem-solving processes. In the automotive industry, they primarily use the 8D, or eight discipline, process. In lean manufacturing, most are familiar with A3. That's a size of paper, but it's also the name of the problem-solving methodology that Toyota and other companies use. Every effective methodology focuses on understanding the problem fully and in context. It's that "measure twice, cut once" theory. In problem solving, you need to measure as many times as it takes until you understand the problem you're trying to solve—and you can state it specifically.

Many manufacturers also know about the 5 Why process of simply asking "why?" until you get to root cause. It's about not coming up with solutions until we know what the problem really is. That's why formal problem-solving methods focus primarily on identifying the root cause. Again, that's a step too many skip.

If we don't agree on the problem, we'll never agree on the solution."

Unfortunately, that just doesn't work. So regardless of what problem-solving methodology you choose, success requires these four elements:

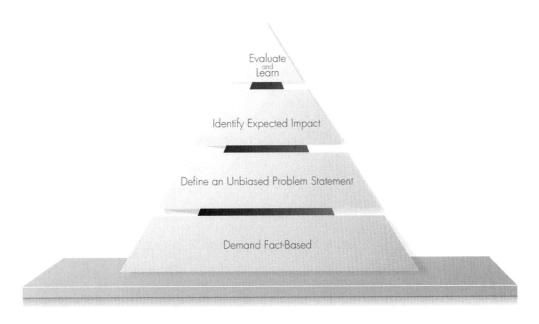

Evaluate and Learn

Identify Expected Impact

Define an Unbiased Problem Statement

Demand Fact-Based

ELIMINATING PROBLEMS

1. Demand fact-based. We all have opinions. But opinions don't really count when it comes to solving problems. We need to deal with facts, and that means leaving the conference room, going out, and finding out what's really going on. It's about collecting data. It's not about making things up or stating beliefs. It doesn't matter how long you've been at your company or in the industry. It doesn't matter how many degrees you have in engineering or anything else. Effective problem solving always requires discipline and fact-based consideration.

2. Define an unbiased problem statement. Far too many people put their proposed solution in the problem statement. For example, they write a problem statement like this: "We have too many employees." Well, I wonder what the solution to that could be? The problem statement is a statement of fact meant to help identify root cause, not to posit solutions. It's critical that the problem statement is unbiased.

3. Identify expected impact. When you identify a solution to a problem, it's important to specifically state how you expect that solution to change the current situation. This is hard to do because everyone's understanding of existing processes is imperfect. If it were perfect, then there wouldn't be any problems. So when you define a solution, take the risk of saying "here's exactly the improvement I think we'll get out of this change." Will the change eliminate the problem, reduce the problem by 50%, or change the outcome to a lessor problem? That thinking will help everyone understand assumptions about processes that may or may not be correct. Without this step, learning from application of your corrective action is limited.

4. Evaluate and learn. Use your statement of expectations, along with the "plan, do, check, adjust" PDCA process, to evaluate your thinking and your understanding. Chances are, the change you made didn't bring about the exact result you had predicted. That's an opportunity to better understand your processes. In fact, every problem is an opportunity to better understand your processes and make them increasingly robust.

STRATEGY #33:

SIMPLIFY, DON'T COMPLICATE

Duct tape was crucial in saving the crew of the Apollo 13 mission when almost everything that could go wrong, did. A toothbrush saved the scientists aboard the International Space Station in 2012 when a malfunction created small metal shavings that would quickly shut down all on-board systems if not removed. Both were complex problems with simple solutions flowing from focused and creative resources.

Clear, shared goals facilitated quick success in these scenarios. Progress sometimes requires more information, and research is appropriate. Other scenarios demand quick creativity. In those cases, fast and probable is more important than slow and certain. Confusing the two can be fatal.

When I explain to people that my pre-consulting career taught me that seemingly disparate challenges are more similar than they are different, some argue that I oversimplify. But it's often better to simplify than to complicate. The ability to see similarities instead of concentrating only on differences helps a manufacturer improve. TRIZ is a problem solving methodology that is based entirely on seeing similarities and is often leveraged to quickly overcome long-standing challenges.

KISS is an acronym developed about 50 years ago and still well-known today. It stands for Keep It Stupid Simple. The term was developed during the skunkworks design of stealth military jets, to reflect the fact that in war, state-of-the-art aircraft must be repairable by average field mechanics using limited tools.

Parts need to be dried? Maybe a hairdryer or the dry cycle on a dishwasher can do the job as well as a fancy industrial oven that requires major capital expenditure. Simplicity requires more open-minded creativity than does development of more complex answers, and often less money. Major challenges are often best met by simple solutions. The principle of Occam's razor should be kept front and center.

As your teams work on solving problems, require them to limit spending and work with urgency, developing more than one potential solution.

This drives more creativity and better thinking than does an unlimited budget and a single option. As they work to prevent problems, insist on similar rules. The goal is a simple solution. There's nothing silly, stupid, or unsophisticated about bringing three men home safely from space using duct tape, if it works. Insist on KISS problem solving every day.

STRATEGY #34:

CREATE THINKERS, NOT DOPPELGANGERS

In school, some teachers give partial credit for doing much of the work correctly on a test; others take an all-or-nothing approach to grading. The first group of students value learning to think; the second value only the "right" answer. I've heard more than once: "I don't want to drive over a bridge designed and built by people who got by on partial credit." I, on the other hand, don't want to drive over a bridge designed and built by folks who only focused on finding the right answer, and don't have anyone around to help them understand the variables not covered in school.

As your team addresses problems, are you most concerned with them reaching the same conclusion that you do, or with the reasoning process they use? As a consultant, it's my job to transfer as much of my knowledge and experience to my client as possible so that when I leave, the progress continues. I've found the only effective way for that to happen is for me to support them as they experiment, and gain understanding. I have to allow them to scrape their knees, while never letting them break a leg.

That's exactly what you need to do to develop a team of creative thinkers, instead of a crew of doppelgangers who mirror your every thought. So how does that happen? You must coach them through their thinking, and let them try things that they believe make sense, even if it's not "your way."

If you need help learning to do this, become familiar with the coaching Kata-a methodology based on the kata process of the martial arts. There are very few problems that haven't been solved in some form, including the challenge of becoming a good coach. Wise men learn from others and this is just another example of that dictum.

People learn more by doing than by simply being told what to do. Your team needs to experiment with their own thinking. Allowing them to build a bridge that will collapse under minimal weight would be dereliction, but never letting them learn how to recognize and consider the many factors involved in safe bridge design would be equally irresponsible.

In fact, letting a model bridge collapse once in a while creates learning and fosters strong problem-solving skills. Making them build the bridge your way, and only your way, doesn't. Create a team of effective problem solvers by encouraging mistakes, out-of-the-box thinking, and autonomy.

//

People learn more by doing than by simply being told what to do."

STRATEGY #35:

MAKE—AND RECOGNIZE— MISTAKES

You order an expensive steak cooked medium rare. It comes out well done. The restaurant's mistake (whether it was the server's fault or the chef's doesn't really matter to you) is irritating and unacceptable.

It's never good when a customer is negatively affected by your organization's mistakes. But mistakes are also a key aspect to learning— and learning leads to effective problem solving and improving.

Let's say an employee at your company has an idea he wants to try, with very specific reasoning and expected outcomes. You encourage him. It turns out he was wrong, but a team invests time in finding out where the logic failed. They learn. They change the experiment, and this time it's successful. More learning. Your organization is better now. Only because you weren't afraid of mistakes.

Internal mistakes are a good thing. If none are made, your organization "must already know everything already"—which means it's both lying to itself and losing ground. So make mistakes. Protect the customer, but make mistakes.

Far too many manufacturers choose to ignore mistakes instead of formally recognizing them. As I work with manufacturers to create lean management systems, I sometimes find that first-level supervisors hesitate to bring problems to the forefront or simply don't recognize them. But as long as yields aren't 100 percent, on-time delivery isn't 100 percent, performance-to-schedule isn't 100 percent, and unplanned machine downtime isn't zero, there must always be problems at an organization.

So why aren't they brought up for discussion? Mistakes aren't a reflection of the supervisor; they're a reflection of the systems and processes in place. The supervisor can't be expected to deal with them alone. It's sometimes difficult to see problems as something to be driven from the business, rather than just "the way things are." Unanswered requests for help can easily reinforce the latter perception.

It has to be not only safe, but encouraged, to discuss problems and mistakes at your organization. Taking the time to truly drive repeat problems from the business has to be a priority for management and support resources. Not all problems are created equal. Priorities for addressing them must be established, communicated, and then executed.

Do your employees see problems? Are they willing to make mistakes visible to others? Or have they been taught to just accept them as "the way things are"? How about you?

STRATEGY #36:

STRIVE ABOVE CONTINUOUS IMPROVEMENT

By now, every company should know that today's level of performance is insufficient for tomorrow's success. Regardless of the details, we're all working to be better through some kind of continuous improvement process. Some of those processes aren't very continuous, and that's a serious problem. But even those that are still face the challenge of basic math.

If your competitor started ahead of you and is improving at the same or greater speed, you'll always be behind. So should you increase the number of week-long kaizen events? Probably not. Most of those are poorly designed and executed and end with more items on the to-do list that don't ever get done than real lasting improvements. You will need both continuous improvement that is truly continuous and the means to identify and execute radical change that competitive leadership requires.

When you're telling others about how you're working to improve your operations, do you describe it as continuous improvement? If so, ask yourself: How is your business better today than it was yesterday, 24 hours ago? How is it better this afternoon than it was this morning, just three or four hours ago? Many organizations believe they are too busy to actually continually improve. Handling day-to-day transactions and responsibilities does take time, but wouldn't it take a lot less time now if you had been continuously improving? Say, for the last month, or year, or decade?

The common excuse from management is: "How do we make time for improvement activities when we're already working overtime?" From the folks doing the actual value-added work for customers, the common complaint is: "They won't give me time to do anything but my job."

Somebody has to break this log jam and it has to be management taking the lead. Improvement thinking has to move from "when we get time" to "when we make time" to "all the time." That's when it becomes part of the job. Not the hourly person's job, but everyone's job.

Do the supervisors in your organization have the skills and the priority to observe work processes, notice waste, and facilitate conversations with the people actually doing the work on how to make things better today? Not at some time in the future; not when we can finally schedule a meeting; but today. Do you have the skills and the priority to develop those skills in your managers? If not, it's time to get started.

If what you're doing isn't getting you there, something very different may well be required. Doing what you do just a bit better may never be good enough. Step back and take a long, hard look. As you work to get better, don't ignore the potential that a major change in your operations may be the only long-term answer. The need to do things entirely differently is unlikely to be seen in an unwavering focus on continuous improvement. Maybe a sharp right turn is in order.

Continuous improvement that's truly continuous is the foundation of long-term competitiveness. But without the addition of step-function performance breakthroughs in areas critical to your market, your company will still lose ground. That's why you must strive above continuous improvement for truly breakthrough improvements to your performance.

What does "breakthrough" mean? It means significant obstructions have been identified and overcome, and performance drastically improved. If you focus on improving processes by solving problems, you've got a great start, but you may still fail to recognize the major obstructions your current process holds.

Every great manufacturer has two or three breakthrough objectives they're focused on right now. They know that attaining those objectives will likely require a significant change in thinking, and they're willing to do that. They know that two or three years may be required to identify obstacles, and design and implement different processes. And they know they must start right now.

Better isn't good enough. Significantly better in ways that benefit the market directly—that's what great companies deliver. Excellent leadership sets breakthrough objectives, and provides the focus and resources to accomplish them. If you haven't defined breakthrough objectives that your teams are working on now, do so soon. Your stakeholders are counting on you.

> **Better isn't good enough. Significantly better in ways that benefit the market directly—that's what great companies deliver."**

CHAPTER 7:
HARNESSING THE POWER OF DATA

"Real knowledge is to know the extent of one's ignorance."
—Confucius

"Then I must have real knowledge, as there's so much I don't know."
—Rebecca Morgan

Many manufacturers are too prone to accepting anecdotes as facts. They make decisions without any data—although they insist they do have data, because someone told them a piece of information. But just because someone genuinely believes something is true, doesn't mean it is. That's the first basic problem that manufacturers face when it comes to data.

The second problem is that some manufacturers have actual data, but they don't trust it. They're unwilling to use the data they have to make real decisions. Instead, the data sits in a storage house. It never becomes useful information.

Defeating these problems is central to surviving in manufacturing today. There are valid approaches to data, and manufacturing leaders must understand, appreciate, and leverage them for key business insights and improvements. And if you know what you're doing, Big Data can be transformational for your organization.

However, the vast majority of manufacturers don't have data analytics skills in-house; after all, engineers aren't statisticians. While the General Electrics of the world have plenty of people who can analyze data correctly, a small to mid-sized company is far less likely to have the resources to deeply understand—and act upon—their data.

This chapter is dedicated to harnessing the power of data, and the first steps you must take to build a solid foundation for a data strategy. The following five strategies will help you navigate a course that truly leverages data to bring your organization closer to operational excellence and long-term success.

STRATEGY #37:

DON'T JUST COLLECT DATA— LEVERAGE IT

My fully-loaded 2012 Audi A6 had an intermittent, frustrating problem since the day I bought it. No diagnostic codes indicated a problem. When I contacted Audi about the issue, their response was infuriating: "It must not really be happening. Our codes would indicate if it were."

That obnoxious response was based on the assumption they had thought of every cause of failure in developing the diagnostic codes. There I was, handing them customer data, and they were ignoring it. Do you have customer data that you're not actively using to improve your product?

Four years after I first reported the issue to Audi, they issued a safety recall for the problem I was experiencing. Why the long delay? Because it only happens on fully loaded vehicles. Audi says it took them four years to recognize and fix the problem because of the limited number of complaints. But you and I both know that even low-level interest and basic statistical analysis could have identified the correlation and led to root-cause analysis.

Is your company only examining customer complaints when they reach a certain established quantity? Ten might not be a statistically valid sample size, but it might well be enough to identify potential correlations. Twenty might be enough to narrow in. Look at problems from the standpoint of your customer, and with the assumption that your buyers aren't crazy. Take their data for what it's worth.

But don't just collect data—leverage it. While a reported problem might be on less than .01 percent of your sales, it's 100 percent to the customer who has it.

You don't have to be a statistician to leverage the data you receive from customers. Ask your internal resources how many of every specific complaint you have, and what the analysis has found so far. Saying you care about quality is only believable if you demonstrate it to each customer. Investing in data collection only has value if you use it.

//
You don't have to be a statistician to leverage the data you receive from customers."

STRATEGY #38:

MASTER SMALL DATA FIRST

We all wish there were a silver bullet to catapult our business to success. Some think it's cheap labor in Asia. Others hedge their bets on Big Data. Let me tell you: Big Data is no silver bullet. Big Data—that ever-expanding velocity, variety, and volume of data being created and stored throughout the world—does have great potential. But it can be a Big Liability, not an asset, without adequate preparation. Master small data first.

Are you effectively leveraging the data you already create and store, known as "small data"? If so, yours is a rare organization, and you're ready for Big Data. Most manufacturers don't have data dictionaries, data maps, or ownership responsibility for data. Without those, employees waste an incredible amount of time looking for what they need. Worse yet, when they find it, they might discover the data is of low quality. Or that there are multiple, disparate versions.

To leverage even small data in improving the quality of strategic decisions requires strong analytical skills, understanding of the issue, and valid timely data. Understanding of the issue without timely data or analytical skills provides qualitative input that can be very valuable, but—keep in mind—qualitative input is also called "opinion." Data without analytical skills or understanding of the issue might be fine for executing transactions, but it's insufficient for drawing any significant conclusions. Effectively leveraging data requires all three components; more on that in Strategy #41: Learn from Data, Big and Small.

Take a step back to look at how you currently manage your data. While storage might be cheap, time wasted looking for data isn't. Nor is misusing data, or using the wrong data. Create a plan for your data, just as you do for any other business asset. Take care of it like you take care of other critical assets. Manage its life cycle and get rid of it when it no longer adds value to your business. Don't create it in the first place unless it adds value. Data should be created with intention, not just as an automatic byproduct of activity.

If you don't do that with your existing data, imagine the mess created by adding the complexity, overabundance, multiple formats, and confusion of Big Data.

An organization of small to mid-sized manufacturing companies asked me several times to deliver a presentation on Big Data to its membership's operations executives. The organization's leadership insisted that the members were craving information about Big Data. I didn't doubt that members said Big Data is important to their success. After all, Big Data is addressed in every industry and business journal of any importance. I just doubted that it was true for most manufacturers of that size.

I finally acquiesced, taking the opportunity to explain to the manufacturing executives that Big Data is very unlikely to help a company that isn't already effectively using the small data that they have. It's hard enough to control and understand the data we create internally—and equally difficult to ensure the data we collect is actually the right information for the problems that we want to solve or the opportunities we want to consider. Adding the complexity of identifying, gathering, understanding, and statistically verifying data from external sources is like trying to run before we can walk.

For example, inventory accuracy in most manufacturers relies on internally controlled transactions and processes, yet is unacceptably low in most cases. How well-understood is that data? How accurate is your measure of supplier performance? Have you been able to improve supplier performance by using that data? What are the root causes of your top three categories of OSHA recordable incidents? Has the data collection and analysis process driven significant prevention activities and have you enjoyed better safety performance?

If you use internal time series data to forecast demand, is the important distinction between customer request date and quantity, promise ship date and quantity, and actual ship date and quantity really understood? Are the processes used to collect the data consistent? Are the statistics of special-cause noise comprehended and applied? Using bad data or misusing good data in making decisions can be disastrous.

My education and work experience includes high-end statistics and math. I value data, but only when it's valid and understood so that it can be wisely used to make decisions. There are a great many questions that Big Data can help answer. When you're confident that you've mastered leveraging the small data that you already have, that's when it's time to move on to using Big Data in running your business. Are you ready?

STRATEGY #39:

USE SMALL DATA WISELY

As we just discovered in Strategy #38 "small data" already exists within your organization and can be extremely powerful when used wisely—even for large organizations. It's easy to think that all big companies are way past small data, and leveraging Big Data every day. But it's simply not true.

For example, ConAgra Foods is a very large group within a very large company. It has multiple divisions, each with multiple facilities. An avalanche of data is created by ConAgra and spread all over the world. You can imagine how difficult it is for anyone to find and understand the nuances of any single piece of internal data they need.

Tim Sasek, manager of human resources and talent analytics at ConAgra Foods, and his team have worked tirelessly to ensure that HR people throughout all operations have the right data at the right time and right place. No Big Data focus; just making sure that the data collected within the company is useful in making business decisions. Sasek emphasized, "We need to get our own house in order before bringing in external data."

Years ago, a centralized team supplied HR data in response to requests from individual HR employees throughout the company. Turnaround time wasn't bad, but even two days can be too long in some cases. Why should they wait at all?

A second issue with providing that raw data to individuals was the resulting flexibility to include and exclude specific data in analysis. That examination might, unfortunately, overlook key aspects that should have been considered. Consistency across facilities was highly unlikely.

ConAgra Foods then moved to a "self-service" model, providing rapidly available, visual summarized data. The goal was effective movement from data to insight to action. By providing an on-demand and easily interpreted summarized view, time to action was significantly reduced. Additionally, common assumptions supported those actions, contributing to consistency across ConAgra Foods.

In reaching that state of "small data management effectiveness," the company considered several data analytics companies before selecting Visier. For some businesses, a simple off-the-shelf package might work, but ConAgra Foods chose this option, as much for the software company's commitment to product development and speed of implementation as for current-state capabilities.

The talent analytics team is far from finished. A small team has responsibility for data quality, and identifying and addressing root causes for systemic problems. As the needs of the organization evolve, so must the collection of data, analysis, and provision of information. In retrospect, Sasek described challenges emanating from the provision of raw data as making the transitions more difficult than necessary. No regrets, just lessons learned.

For your company, a specialized analytics package might not be necessary. For your business, providing raw data to be used as chosen by individuals might be the right step. But there's a lesson to be learned from the ConAgra Foods example: Before you go crazy chasing Big Data, make sure you understand your own data and use it wisely. That process takes time, but it's time well-invested.

STRATEGY #40:

ESTABLISH A BIG DATA STRATEGY

So your organization has mastered small data. You use small data wisely to make effective business decisions, and it's fully understood by individuals across the spectrum of your company. Now what? You might be ready for Big Data, and it's time to establish a solid strategy to leverage it.

If you aim to use Big Data to help you find out what's real, and not to prove points, then you'll find it powerful in improving strategic and operational decisions. Every year or so, a new "silver bullet" enters the business lexicon. Just in case the new concept really holds the key to future success, the responsible executive must learn and assess this solution for valued use. Big Data continues to be described as a silver bullet, and it's only gathering more steam. What is it? And why should you care?

Big Data refers to all that data you're collecting internally (e.g., employee card swipes, equipment readings, incoming calls) or that's being collected externally (e.g., cell phone locations, website visits, apps like Waze or Belly), via technology in both cases. It may reside in emails, in databases, or in application software. In its current state, it's a long way from being information, but there are likely a few needles in that haystack. As technology proliferates and data storage costs fall, the collection of data will continue to expand. You need a strategy to convert Big Data to information that facilitates better business decisions.

First, there are questions you have that require information to answer well. Amazon provides a well-known example of this. Without a commitment to fast, accurate delivery of customer orders, Amazon would be just another distributor. But as part of that company's commitment to pressing the limits, it recently opened a pilot warehouse in New York City promising one-hour delivery of a specified group of items, within a certain radius. Without data on ordering patterns, business density, and traffic patterns, this pilot project couldn't succeed. With it, the company will learn a lot as it moves closer to its goals.

There are also those questions you don't even know you have, but that the data can point you to. Public examples are harder to find, but consider your own business. You might find a correlation between unplanned equipment shutdowns and purchases of maintenance, repair, and operating supplies. Or you'll see connections between those shutdowns and the absentee of a particular employee. Whether using external or internal data, there's no telling where it can take you. One place you don't want Big Data to take you is down a rabbit hole. Not all data will be useful, and no data is unbiased information without a trained mind looking at it.

Statistics don't lie; statisticians do. If you want to use data to verify an opinion, you'll likely be able to find data to do so. That doesn't make it true. To effectively use Big Data, you need resources with an understanding of the data (definitions, timing, reliability, etc.) as well as statistics. You must also recognize that Big Data isn't a silver bullet—but it certainly is important and worth your time.

As you begin to incorporate a Big Data strategy into your business, start by considering these four fundamental questions:

1. What questions do I need to answer, and what data will help me do that?
2. Is the data available reliable enough to use in drawing conclusions?
3. How can I understand the data definitions well enough to use the data intelligently?
4. How do I utilize qualitative information? Or do I?

Big Data will continue to mushroom as technology use expands and storage prices fall. But data is not information. Sorting through all the data that's available to find the nuggets of importance to your business is no simple task. However, it's a task every business that has mastered small data should begin to consider.

One place you don't want Big Data to take you is down a rabbit hole."

STRATEGY #41:
LEARN FROM DATA, BIG AND SMALL

So many manufacturers are just gung-ho excited about the potential of Big Data. Unfortunately, those same people are rarely fully leveraging the data they have. Let me share with you how to successfully learn from data, whether that data is big or small. First, consider these three interrelated competencies, each of which requires time and effort to master:

LEARNING FROM DATA

1. Guess   2. Irrelevant   3. Unarmed   4. SUCCESSFUL

When only one of these competencies rules the day, learning doesn't happen. And the mutual existence of any two of these three competencies is, sadly, also of limited value.

If your organization understands the issue and has the right data at the right time and place, but doesn't have strong analytical skills at its disposal, then you're still just guessing. You might now be guessing supplemented by numbers manipulated to reinforce your opinion, but it's no more valid than opinions without data.

If your organization has the data and the analytical skills but doesn't understand the issue it's facing, then analysis is largely irrelevant. And with both analytical skills and an understanding of the issue, but without the right data available, your team is simply unarmed.

It's only with all three competencies—understanding the issue, the right data at the right time and place, and strong analytical skills—that your team can successfully learn from and leverage data.

My best clients, and all great organizations, are operating in the intersection of these three proficiencies. They progress by improving their mastery in all three circles, and therefore they keep learning more and more. Only then is Big Data a real possibility. It's something to get excited about—but until then, remember to focus on how your company best can leverage the data you already have.

CHAPTER 8:
EMBRACING TECHNOLOGY—ALL IN

"Innovation distinguishes between a leader and a follower."
—Steve Jobs

"Innovation requires imagination, creativity, and a willingness
to experience failure as key to the learning process.
Leading organizations foster that environment."
—Rebecca Morgan

In many manufacturing businesses, technology is considered a methodology to eliminate people. The more these companies embrace technology, the fewer people they expect to employ at the end of the day. This couldn't be a more misguided way of looking at technology in manufacturing. If your reason for embracing technology is to eliminate people from your organization, you've got the wrong goal in mind.

Technology exists to help you understand how you can develop—and deliver—new and better products to your customers. You should embrace technology because it adds value to what you already do, or what you need to do, and makes you a better organization.

Too many organizations often have no expertise in choosing the right technology with the right capabilities to address the problem at hand. They go look at some robots, say, "That one looks cool!" and end up wasting money on useless technology.

Don't be one of those manufacturers. Instead, establish a technology strategy that is part of your operations strategy—you can't approach it haphazardly. Begin to view technology as improving the productivity of your people, not eliminating people. Without technology, you can't remain competitive. The following four strategies will show you how to embrace technology at your manufacturing business—all in.

STRATEGY #42:

LEVERAGE THE "INTERNET OF THINGS"

If you think your business won't be affected by the Internet of Things, think again. The Internet of Things (IoT) is defined as "the network of physical devices, vehicles, buildings, and other items—embedded with electronics, software, sensors, actuators, and network connectivity that enable these objects to collect and exchange data." In other words, it's all about communication. If you're not in the communication business now, you soon will be—IoT will see to that.

You might have heard that IoT is the new frontier in manufacturing and, without it, your company will die a painful death. That might be a bit hyperbolic, but IoT is definitely the way of the future. Just as every company of any size has an ERP system today, almost all manufacturers will soon be involved in IoT. Understanding why and how will be instrumental to making IoT an asset—and not a heavy chain that drags you down.

How can you make sure that IoT is a positive for your company? Think about MRP and ERP systems. We all know stories about companies that invested millions in cash and resources to implement the latest and greatest, only to be unable to ship at "go-live." That's not usually the direct fault of the ERP software, but rather a lack of understanding of needs and of the software itself.

Companies that implement and operate those systems well had an excellent project plan that reflected defined needs and lots of testing with real data. Those that took shortcuts, knowingly or not, suffered the slings and arrows of outrageous fortune.

Now think about Big Data—the precursor to IoT. Very few companies have believable and timely internal data and those that do often fail to analyze it. Yet, as we explored in the previous chapter, many organizations rush to become involved with Big Data, not knowing quite why. If your own "small data" is questionable, clean it up. If it's trustworthy, leverage it. Then, when you have a plan with defined needs, go after Big Data. It holds a million stories. You must read the right ones and not get sidetracked by all the interesting but irrelevant distractions. The same goes for IoT. Today, we want all our equipment to not only talk to us, but to each other, to our systems, and to our products in the field. And do it with data. We love that Tesla can update options on our car via download rather than taking it to a dealer—but think who else might be interacting with your car with evil intention.

If you plan to internalize IoT, start with an understanding of why, and of the resources you'll need to make it work for you and your customers. If you think internet and cloud security are a challenge, you haven't seen anything yet. This work won't be fit for the casual IT department, nor a part-time "when I find the time" approach. As with any other new technology and service offering, a well-founded strategy is a must. Don't just start leveraging IoT. Start with a plan.

If you're not in the communication business now, you soon will be—IoT will see to that."

STRATEGY #43:
MARRY TECH WITH OPERATIONS

Bill Gates famously predicted a computer in every home, much to the amusement of then-current-day business gurus. His vision of the inevitable was clear and accurate.

In 1985, Steve Jobs said that the internet, then in its infancy, was the reason people would buy computers—to connect with others. Jobs' Apple subsequently changed the product model from desktop computers to phones and tablets.

Simultaneously, machine designers began to build in automation and information systems. ERP systems grew from basic MRP programs, based on the premise that more information, faster, is better. Now we see the availability and potential of Big Data, with the Internet of Things fast approaching. It's time to marry technology with your operations, fully and as seamlessly as possible.

IT expertise has become a required competency for every manufacturer, regardless of size or industry. The essential proficiencies are increasingly diverse. The expert who can protect your systems from hackers is unlikely to adroitly provide application expertise. It's improbable that this same professional can write software to control your equipment and determine when and what to communicate.

Information prowess is fast becoming an additional prerequisite to operating a successful manufacturing business.

We worry about the shortage of experienced equipment operators. We lament the lack of experienced warehousemen. Those skills we know how to train. Providing the technology development and information selection and analysis skills that are demanded is a different story. And it's one you need to start paying attention to.

Like it or not, all manufacturers—even the small ones—are in the technology and communication business. Every manufacturer is in the rapid-prototyping and quick-learning cycle business.

Manufacturing operations and technology must be married; and there will be no divorce. Each is growing quickly, and often in different directions. The relationship can be rocky. Independent decision making, outside of strategy, will only make it worse. Many will need caring counseling, discovering where each aspect must prosper and where each is committed to excess. While to some it might feel like an arranged marriage, everyone must learn to make it work.

STRATEGY #44:

STAY AHEAD OF THE DIGITAL CURVE

Control over your sold products is about to end—unless you act now. Additive manufacturing (3D printing) is a double-edged sword that impacts every manufacturer. While it enables rapid inexpensive product development and designs that couldn't be manufactured using existing technologies, it also allows millions of people around the world to easily replicate your parts or products without your knowledge.

As a result, intellectual property (IP) challenges are exploding. Supply chain challenges are exploding. Opportunities to drastically improve, or completely lose, your service-parts business are exploding. Warranty cost management demands are exploding. To combat these challenges, and effectively stay ahead of the 3D curve, take the following five steps:

1. Define your 3D controls strategy for quality, outsourcing, service parts, warranty, and IP protection.
2. Design IP controls into important parts to complicate unauthorized 3D printing.
3. Strictly control parts files, internally and externally. Emailing these is like emailing your social security number. Allowing suppliers to share these is inviting fraud. Sending files to get multiple quotes is akin to posting on Facebook.
4. Communicate the risks and your prevention actions to customers. Some might want to save money, but most want fast, authentic service parts. Consider creating controlled additive manufacturing capability near remote customer enclaves.
5. Implement warranty processes that work well for legitimate requests and identify illicit ones.

Illegitimate use of 3D printing makes identity theft seem scarce and benign by comparison. And 3D is only the surface of a host of similar technology innovations that will soon take manufacturing by storm.

Think those kids playing video games are wasting time? The curious ones are developing skills that will change our world. Augmented reality (AR) has entered the sales and marketing arena, and is showing great results. Whether it's an app that shows what you would look like with that hair cut and color you've been considering, or one that let's you see how your kitchen would look with that new wallpaper, the technology is now embedded in common buying decisions.

AR is changing education in ways that could have made me somewhat interested in chemistry—and that's a real accomplishment! One tool shows the periodic table elements as blocks. As the student brings blocks together, the chemistry experiment takes place on screen. We can see what happens without endangering the entire neighborhood. Would it help the user of your product if they easily could see how it fits, works, processes, etc.? Maybe one of those gamers is going to change how you train employees, or alter the way you sell. As AR thinking moves into operations, it might not only change what the market expects of your product, but also how you design and make products, ensure quality, store items, and ship them. Grand Theft Auto V, anyone?

//
Think those kids playing video games are wasting time? The curious ones are developing skills that will change our world."

STRATEGY #45:

NO TECH FOR THE SAKE OF TECH

I once had a client who insisted on using material requirements planning (MRP) to execute short-term scheduling of suppliers and the shop floor, despite the fact that MRP doesn't do that well at all. It can't. And then the owner was upset about late orders and too much work in process.

His argument for using MRP? He wanted to use the tools he already had instead of learning new ones. Should you use the tools you already have or use the most appropriate techniques? The answer seems obvious to me: Just because you have a screwdriver doesn't mean you should use it to cut down a tree. Get a saw. Or hire someone with a saw. And do that only when you're sure the tree needs to be cut down.

This question of technology, tools, and simple solutions matters now more than ever. The "fourth industrial revolution" is all about advanced statistics and electronic wizardry. Like Big Data, it's a great theory, and is useful to many organizations that have both the need and skillsets required. But for the average company, it's like putting your 16-year-old in a Formula One racecar. It won't end well. At least not until he learns he's not invincible and he learns to drive well.

"The Jetsons," "Star Wars," and "Back to The Future" whetted our appetites for advanced technology. Current blockbuster movies continue to build that interest. It's easy to become enamored with technologies at trade shows or those we see in someone else's operations. While the image of robots intermingling with employees can be exciting, the real issue is whether it's profitable for your business.

"Pick and place" robots have been used for years in manufacturing to replace dangerous, monotonous, or error-prone human activities. This type of equipment is especially valuable in high-speed, high-quantity, high-precision placement. The caveat, however, is that the process must be extremely precise for an entry-level robot to actually work.

Low-priced robots require complete predictability of where, when, and how. They can't hunt around, figure out when to act, or tweak things that aren't quite right. That requirement for definitive processes is a significant challenge for most small manufacturers.

Unsophisticated robots aren't cheap. Investing $10,000 to $40,000 in a simple option is a significant decision for small manufacturers. Moreover, the purchase price is only the first of several costs to be incurred. Detailed programming and equipment maintenance might require new internal skills or outside contracting. Programs will likely need to be revised whenever product shape, production processes, or equipment locations change.

So is a robot a bad idea for a small manufacturer? Not at all, if you've thought it through and can effectively support it. In fact, it can have a positive impact on the business beyond the initial justification. Consider these four questions before spec'ing your own R2-D2:

1. Does the work actually need to be done at all?
Automating work steps that shouldn't be required in the first place makes no sense. If time is wasted looking for tools or materials, you'll need to fix that before installing robots. The equipment must be programmed to know where to go, when. As much as we might like it, there's no "figure it out on your own" button on low-priced robots. Lean manufacturing methodologies can ensure tools, parts, and information are well-located to support the worker. I encourage you to quickly research "5S." Well implemented, the concept will reduce "now, where is it?" wandering around—and make robotics possible.

2. Is the work so elementary that a human shouldn't be wasting his life doing it anyway?
Your employees are capable of contributing value far in excess of moving items from Point A to Point B. Utilizing a robot for basics and people for activities and decisions that require intellect can greatly improve job satisfaction and reduce turnover.

3. Could the robot supplement other material handling equipment you use? If you currently depend on tow motors, hand jacks, or similar devices to move product, a robot could augment that capacity and reduce waiting time. Perhaps the robot could lift and hold heavy items, allowing workers additional angles of access.

4. Does the work require judgment that an inexpensive robot can be programmed to have? Make sure you understand the seemingly small decisions your employees are making every day as they complete their work. If those conditions can be standardized, do so, whether for your employees or a robot.

Too many organizations insist on using technology just because they've already paid for it, or because they want to have the latest and greatest tool available. Here's some advice: Run your business. Identify the problems that are preventing your success. Discover root cause. Determine how best to drive the problems from your business. Don't just acquire technology for the sake of acquiring technology.

CHAPTER 9:
YOUR COMPETITIVE ADVANTAGE

"Progress always involves risk; you can't steal
second base and keep your foot on first base."
—Robert Quillen

"No great base runner operates out of fear; nor does any great
business. Manage risks and head for second."
—Rebecca Morgan

Everyone talks about "competitive advantage," but few manufacturers have a clear idea of what it means for them. Manufacturers tend to look internally when thinking about their competitive advantage, focusing on a particular piece of equipment or the speed of certain operational capabilities. They look at how those strengths give them an advantage over the competition. But real competitive advantage is different.

Real competitive advantage is the advantage that your customers gain by doing business with you instead of with your competitors.

How does your company give your customers an advantage over their competition? How do you enable them to outshine others in their market space? That's the true definition of your competitive advantage.

The capabilities, products, and services that you provide to your customers all must help them increase the value they provide to their customers. Those advantages can take many forms, and require an understanding of the needs and wants of your customers' markets. Price becomes an afterthought when the significance of your contribution is integral to your customers' success.

This chapter is devoted to the idea of competitive advantage. The following four strategies touch upon key approaches to strengthening your company's competitive advantage.

STRATEGY #46:

MAKE YOUR COMMODITY STAND OUT

A commodity offering, by definition, is undifferentiated. A consumer has no reason to choose one commodity offering over another, other than price. But by making small changes to materials, processing, or marketing, you can make your commodity distinct—and earn a higher price for it.

For example, I recently went to the market to buy low-sodium tomato sauce. There were three brands and two container types that all said "no salt added" on the front. Had I not read the labels carefully, I would have purchased either the cheapest option, or the brand I knew best. However, the details showed that the actual quantity of sodium per comparable serving varied widely. I bought the one with the lowest sodium content—but only because I took the time to figure out there was a real difference. Clearly, consumers of this "no salt added" product care about sodium content—but they might not suspect distinctions among the different choices.

A label noting the extremely and relatively low salt level could increase sales simply by making it easier to know. Perhaps minor process or ingredient changes could reduce sodium levels to the point of "no sodium" labeling, which could further differentiate the product. Know where your offering can be easily differentiated in ways the customer cares about. If it can pay for itself, make the change. Otherwise you're giving your competitors the chance to do it first.

As a manufacturer, your worldwide competition never sleeps. Whether your competitors are simply in different time zones, or they're large companies that operate 24/7/365, when you go home, they're still working to unseat you from your best customers.

Terror, fear, and anxiety might seem logical under these circumstances, but they're hardly useful. The realization that what was once good enough is no longer, understanding that currently accepted performance will underwhelm in the near future, and knowing you are committed to manufacturing greatness and the constant work it

requires are all important to getting a good night's sleep.
The best companies, and those that survived the last major downturn, certainly are doing something right. They're truly committed to "every one, every day" as they focus on increasing value to the market. They know strong leadership that shows the way forward with consistency and fortitude will stay ahead of the lesser competitors nipping at their heels.

If you're satisfied to be one of those lesser competitors, you must learn to survive on the crumbs left by others. If you're one with strong leadership and effective never-ending commitment to excellence, rest well. The competition might never sleep, but you can.

//
As a manufacturer, your worldwide competition never sleeps."

STRATEGY #47:

EARN YOUR CUSTOMERS' TRUST

Repeat customers who are true fans of your business are hard to come by, easy to lose, and costly to replace. So how do you get them—and keep them? Understand what your target market really cares about, and then deliver consistency both in perception and performance. Neither alone is sufficient.

By way of example, Wal-Mart's customers are primarily rural with limited alternatives, or urban with a focus on low prices. News of its products being produced in foreign sweatshops employing children won't harm their sales, because the savings perception is, by necessity, more important than ethical issues for its market. But if Wal-Mart ever lost its market perception of being "reliably inexpensive," sales would plummet. Its operations management must deliver on that expectation, or else.

Apple created the first "cool" cell phone and its entire market. Now, their competitors work to create a market perception that iPhones are for old people, not hip young adults. Equipment performance isn't unique among manufacturers, so retail outlets, buzz, and delivery-as-promised with easy data transfer must meet expectations.

While Fed-Ex and UPS have both faced legal issues relating to knowingly carrying illegal drugs for delivery, both maintain a high-quality reputation. Why? Their stature is preferred over the poorly perceived US Post Office.

If perception is so critical to earning your customers' trust, what's the role of performance? Simply put, performance is about delivering on the perceptions that are important to your market. We trust our grocery stores, our drug stores, and our automobile dealerships to sell us legitimate products. If we ever discovered that Honda brand cars run a risk of being black-market fakes, that company couldn't recover.

We expect "high-end stores" to sell legitimate products made in production environments that comply with ethics and laws.

If Nordstrom's supply chain were determined to include knockoffs made in sweatshops, that retailer would go out of business.

In order to earn your customers' trust—and keep it—you can't be sloppy, make assumptions, or abdicate responsibility to suppliers. As a manufacturer, it's your job to deliver on brand promise, including on the perception you've created in the market. To do otherwise would be to betray the trust of your customers.

STRATEGY #48:

CONSTANTLY ADAPT TO CHANGE

If only all American manufacturers acted as if Charles Darwin's declaration were true: "It is not the strongest of the species that survives, nor the most intelligent that survives. It is the one that is the most adaptable to change." While some companies constantly work at becoming more competitive every single day, others continue to act as if 1950 is right around the corner. The manufacturing world changes daily, with customer expectations and global competition on the rise. If you want your organization to survive and strengthen its competitive advantage, you must constantly adapt to change.

As market winds change direction, it's critical that you develop the ability to recognize which winds are gentle breezes that will come and go, and which are violent gales about to leave destruction in their wake.

In manufacturing, commodity prices vary day to day, with the occasional unexpected wild swing. Exchange rates fluctuate with the occasional devaluation. Technology and material science continually evolve and, once in a while, a disruptive advance enters the market. Availability of skilled resources can be inconsistent—and due in no small part to prior offshoring, it's becoming a threatening challenge to many companies. Business processes function effectively within a range, but active intervention is sometimes required. Scalable processes are more robust than those dependent on brute force, but market changes can require redesign of even the most flexible processes.

The factors I've listed above are wide-ranging, but it's crucial that manufacturers can adapt to them all. Detection systems and triggers are essential to navigating business winds. Equally important is an openness to major shifts that can influence the flexibility of your organization. Let's take a look at some companies who've failed to adapt to change over the years—and others who continue to rise to the occasion.

First up is Blackberry. This company stuck with its "our smartphone is for business, the other ones are just toys" mantra for entirely too long. As a result, Blackberry is a largely broken company with a fractured market.

Sony has a similar story with its once-ubiquitous Walkman. The Walkman changed how the world listened to music. Unfortunately, Sony was so inflexible about the Walkman's role in the market that it couldn't handle the subsequent evolution of portable electronics.

That's where ever-adaptable Apple stepped in. They took the concept of portable music much further with the iPod, and changed the way music was purchased with iTunes. Applications like Spotify came on the scene to further change the financial model of music, but so far Apple has been sufficiently flexible to adapt well to those shifting winds.

Likewise, publishing has experienced a revolution in recent years. Surviving companies in that industry recognize that they're now in the information distribution business, not the publishing business.

The manufacturing industry will soon undergo similarly major strategic changes in products and business models as sustainability becomes more important to our markets. Scalable processes alone won't keep companies afloat. Consider this an advanced warning of the storm of the century.

In fact, the economics of the manufacturing industry are changing right now. China might represent the best-known example of differing ethics (a.k.a., respect for copyright and patents) affecting manufacturers. Digitization is everywhere, which enables the 3D printer to increasingly meet the "I want it, and I want it now" aspect of demand. New distribution channels are evolving, influenced by the need for cost reduction and the expectation of immediate supply.

If you assume your industry is immune from these shifts, you're wrong. Whether B2B or B2C, your world is morphing into something you haven't faced before.

Whether B2B or B2C, your world is morphing into something you haven't faced before."

New materials, processes, technologies, product innovation, and socioeconomic factors will transform what's made, how, and where it's done. For some observers, these coming changes indicate the impending demise of manufacturing as we know it. But until evidence suggests that materialistic values and modern conveniences are being rejected worldwide, my belief in the survival of manufacturing will remain firm.

Darwin made an important point about change. Note that he said surviving species are "adaptable" to change, not that they "can run from" change. Keep your organization adaptable, and your competitive advantage will grow.

STRATEGY #49:

ALWAYS FINISH STRONG®

All the way back in Strategy #8: Finish What You Start, I told you about my trademarked Finish Strong® concept, composed of the following five elements:

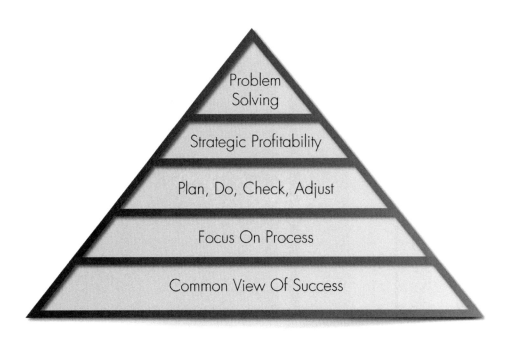

Problem Solving

Strategic Profitability

Plan, Do, Check, Adjust

Focus On Process

Common View Of Success

The Finish Strong® Path To Profitability

The idea of Finish Strong® is just as important to competitive advantage as it is to profitability and strong leadership. The basic thrust of Finish Strong®—that companies must create a process by which they can repeatedly, consistently, and reliably finish what they start—is central to market competitiveness. Without a strong finish, customers will never know who you are. Your products will never reach the right market. And you most certainly won't rise above the competition.

Be honest: Had you ever heard of Giacomo before he beat 50:1 odds to win the 2005 Kentucky Derby? He's gone down in history, and all because of a strong finish in a race. My own Cleveland Cavaliers just won the 2016 NBA championship after being down 3 games to 1 in the Finals. They came back to force a game seven and won it at the end with a strong finish. What does that have to do with your company? Simply put, a strong finish can differentiate you from your competition, leaving a positive and lasting impression in the minds of your customers. In short, it can make you a winner.

Most builders and tradesmen take their professions very seriously. They want to be the best at what they do. Unfortunately, many don't see administration, documentation, project management, and demobilization as work that demands excellence as well. Yet your customers do. They expect it from you.

Let's consider two businesses with equally talented general contractors, GC-A and GC-B, each working on projects for Developer D. GC-A begins the job with a full crew, off to a rousing start. As field changes occur, GC-A makes mental notes, promising to update as-built documentation later. He focuses on communicating the changes to his crew. As the target completion date approaches, GC-A peels his crew off to begin work on other jobs. He leaves behind a skeleton crew to handle loose ends and final inspection items.

Unfortunately, the skeleton crew doesn't have the skills to handle everything. GC-A tells his workers, who've since moved on to other jobs, to go back over and finish those items whenever they get the chance. The tenant can move in anyway; after all, the building is "substantially complete." Some gear is left at the site, so it can be moved directly to the next job. The tenant shouldn't really mind.

When GC-A calls to arrange final payment, Developer D reminds him of the undelivered as-built documents, the incomplete final inspection items, and the equipment still sitting at the site. "The tenant is in, isn't he?" argues GC-A, believing he's done another excellent job. Developer D barely recalls GC-A's strong start. He remembers only GC-A's failure to finish.

On the other hand, GC-B is working on an unrelated project for that same developer. He shows up on the scheduled start date ready to begin. Every member of the relatively small crew seems to understand the plans, have needed supplies, and know exactly what to do. As field changes occur, GC-B discusses them with the crew while he updates his records. He knows that field changes often cause schedule delays, cost overruns, and confusion. To avoid those problems, he's developed a real-time method of tracking changes, including the reason and the anticipated resource and time impact, which updates as-built documentation as work is completed.

As the project progresses, the crew grows. GC-B's experience has shown that the various trades working together as a job nears completion can prevent and resolve problems in cooperation much better than they can working sequentially. As issues are identified, the appropriate experts are there to address them. When the job is complete, all gear is removed from the site. The job is complete—truly complete—before the tenant moves in. The as-built drawings are complete when the project is complete, not weeks or months later.

GC-B finishes strong. He has done what he said he would do, when he said he would do it. His customer doesn't have to nag, beg, or threaten to get what he bought. Which general contractor do you think Developer D will use next time? Whichever one is cheaper, you say? Don't count on it. Anyway, there's no reason to believe GC-B has higher costs. A well-run company usually has lower costs than its ineffective competitors. And don't think that the developer doesn't recognize the cost he incurs in dealing with a supplier like GC-A.

What's the moral of the story? Understand what your customer values. Understand what you've agreed to deliver. Understand the reputation you're building through the footprints you leave behind. The winner of any race always comes from among those who finish. The winner never comes from among those who come close to finishing, but then move on to a different race. Finish, and finish strong. You have to finish to remain in the competition.

CHAPTER 10:
THE FUTURE AT WORK

"Those who cannot change their minds cannot change anything."
—George Bernard Shaw

"Future success requires willingness to change minds—starting with our own."
—Rebecca Morgan

People will always want things. And as long as people want things, there will always be manufacturing. But for a manufacturing company to be successful in the long-term, the leaders at its helm must continuously look into the future. Will the products your company makes be needed in the future—or will that need be eliminated? Answering this question is key to making sure your company continues to design in-demand products. It's also critical to ensuring you can meet the future needs of your markets.

In manufacturing, planning for the future is not only about marketing; it's also about engineering, operations, and leadership. To prepare your organization for a successful future, all three of these components must be top-of-mind in the C-suite. So must innovation. Simply repeating successful past approaches isn't enough to propel your company forward into the future. That mentality will cripple any manufacturer. Instead, it's about a constant, forward-looking push to make your strategic vision a reality.

The final chapter of this book explores nine powerful strategies to guide you on this path. From effective hiring strategies and the importance of pioneering design and sustainability, to building a company culture of innovation and assessing market needs, you'll learn ways to strengthen your organization's future.

STRATEGY #50:

IDENTIFY, ASSESS, AND MANAGE RISK

The West Coast port slowdown. Internet hacks that disable equipment. Falling capacity on next-flight-out airplanes. A tractor-trailer accident that destroys your products en route to your customers. Snowstorms that block roads and knock out power. As Saturday Night Live's Roseanne Roseannadanna warned us, "It's always something." Murphy's Law is a law, after all. That's why the first step to creating a viable future for your organization is to ensure that risk identification, assessment, and management are integrated within your operations strategy.

Your operations strategy creates the primary plan for profitably supporting your company's brand promise. It contains the framework for how operational decisions are to be made. Done well, this can be the difference between long-term success and failure. But even the best-laid plans go awry—and so risk management and contingency planning are critical components of a strong operations strategy. As speed requirements accelerate, globalization trends continue, and both man and nature maintain unpredictable behaviors, preparing to act within the framework of your operations strategy is increasingly important.

A key part of creating your operations strategy must be assessing both the probability and severity of risks. While no strategy precludes risk entirely, different strategies can manage risk to levels that are acceptable to individual organizations. It's how those interruptions are handled that distinguishes the best companies from the rest. And how well those interruptions are handled is a direct function of preparation.

Big disasters like the 2011 Japanese earthquake and tsunami can only be overcome by the cooperation of major organizations. If metaphorical bridges have been burned, any recovery will be negatively impacted. Stay friends with your competition. Smaller disasters like record-setting blizzards in the Northeast United States require prioritization, communication, and alternatives that are already conceived. You must ensure access to that information despite the disturbance.

Predictable interruptions like the West Coast port slowdown as a prelude to a contract negotiation, or power outages in wild weather, should be tactically defined under your operations strategy. Here are five actions you can take to minimize the impact of Murphy's Law on your organization:

1. Review your operations strategy—and if you don't have one, draft an outline to reflect your organization's current thinking and behaviors.
2. Identify the top three to five risks in each aspect of your operations, such as supply chain, manufacturing quality, and engineering. Rank each risk in terms of probability and severity of impact to your organization and your customers.
3. Document any mitigation plans already prepared or implemented for each identified risk.
4. Create a risk heat map, or use a similar tool to visibly document your current situation.
5. Prioritize the risks for mitigation or alternatives—and get started.

"It won't happen to me!" is honorably optimistic, but is not an effective way to identify, assess, and manage risk. Unfortunately, it's the prevailing mindset of manufacturers when it comes to all sorts of business risk. I see a remarkable amount of denial in the C-suite around the likelihood of very common interruptions impacting their organizations. Failure to seriously consider potential problems is a fatal flaw when it comes to effective future planning for manufacturers.

The best example of this widespread issue has to do with security. While no one is unaware of the frequency—and dire ramifications—of stolen passwords and stolen identities, most manufacturers still turn a blind eye to online security risks. Over the past several years, the quantity of malicious emails sent from obviously hacked email accounts has steadily grown. But it's rare that the recipients of those emails ever change their passwords in response. No wonder insurance premiums keep climbing.

Anticipate that the widespread problem of hacking might affect your organization—even if it never has before. Change all your passwords regularly and use more secure quantities and combinations of characters.

Password software is helpful, affordable, and will do the job better than sticky notes. Utilize transaction notification alerts with all credit cards, both business and personal.

And what about identifying more unlikely risks than cyber hacks—such as factory explosions? Consider the families and businesses that were affected by the massive explosion in the Chinese port city of Tian Jinn. While many of the surrounding operations may have safely stored and handled hazardous materials, clearly at least one of them did not. While I'm as optimistic as the next person, I do believe in awareness, prevention, contingencies, and mitigation planning.

 If you're sure that your operations are handling hazardous material safely, it's time to start talking with your industrial neighbors. An industrial park safety group is one of many alternatives for cooperation. If your operations are on a dead-end street, ensure egress alternatives from the area are available and clearly marked.

I hope nothing bad happens to your business, or to your neighboring business, but blind optimism is not the way to build a sustainable future for your company. Assume the glass is leaking—and know how you'll capture the water if it really is.

//
Assume the glass is leaking—and know how you'll capture the water if it really is."

STRATEGY #51:

FOSTER INNOVATION

These days, focus on innovation is a reflection of the quickening pace of change in expectations. Speed is not enough; vitality requires acceleration. Change alone is not enough; innovation is required. And as the leader of your company, it's up to you to foster innovation throughout the ranks.

Manufacturing companies must both respond to and create advancing technologies and customer needs. The challenge is to discover what will keep your business vibrant two, five, and ten years from now—and beyond. Innovation provides a cornerstone to that future. There are three primary arenas of innovation to consider:

1. Product Innovation
2. Process Innovation
3. Design Innovation

It's important to understand what each type of innovation can mean for your company. Product innovation offers the potential protection of intellectual property and patents. If you can develop a product the market wants and bring it to market quickly, you may receive long-term, protected dividends.

While process innovations are theoretically easier to copy and therefore bring less long-term competitive advantage, they're nonetheless worthy pursuits. In fact, process innovations are a primary method of attacking overhead and indirect costs and can significantly impact customer interactions. Dell is known to have capitalized phenomenally well on process innovation. The computer company's financial success stems from its highly regarded logistics and supply chain management, which enables it to use customers' money to pay suppliers.

Apple is a notable leader in design innovation. The company has been skilled, especially in recent years, at bringing to market technological products that capture the imagination of its target markets in both functionality and styling, and supporting them with equally well-designed marketing. One could certainly argue that Apple excels in both product and design innovation.

Successful companies cultivate a corporate culture that embraces "intelligent risk-taking." They know that no failures probably mean they missed some great opportunities. It's the challenge of leadership to determine where innovation can best provide the fulcrum to propel your company forward. It's time to put your company under the microscope and then look at the market through a telescope to determine the current best path to a fertile future. If your products or services solve real problems in the market, someone else is working on eliminating the problems or solving them differently. They want what you have.

To foster true innovation at your company, here are six behaviors to cultivate:

1. Accept that change is necessary but not sufficient; innovation is required.
2. Engage formal and informal leaders to visit, read, and listen to external stimulators and trends to gain conviction to support an innovative culture within the company.
3. Examine current processes and systems to identify where they hinder or support innovation; at a minimum, utilize that awareness productively.
4. Exploit creative tools, such as storyboarding, forced conflict, or morphological analysis, by training all employees how to use a few selected ones well.
5. Leverage relationships with the innovative and interested among both your supply and customer bases.
6. Pay close attention to your customers. Watch how they use your products or services. Ask them for feedback. Create solutions for the problem they describe, but also the larger problem you see causing it.

If your company is already a successful innovator, congratulations. If not, consider your competitive marketplace a fast-approaching perfect storm. Do nothing, and your company shares the fate of the Andrea Gail. Or choose to safely ride the wind and the waves by encouraging a culture that supports innovation and change.

Internal skills can be developed, and augmented with external relationships. Working with customers, non-customers, competitors, suppliers, or others to develop new solutions can help set the course for the future of your company.

"
Successful companies cultivate a corporate culture that embraces "intelligent risk-taking"."

STRATEGY #52:

LEARN, SHARE, AND GROW

Innovation is no longer the purview of the brilliant, focused individual in his basement. It's quickly becoming too complex and demanding even for the mid-sized or large business with multiple engineering departments. Development of smart products using new materials, technologies, and manufacturing methods requires an abundance of knowledge and resources that won't be met by a single organization, nor with traditional outsourcing.

The Association for Manufacturing Excellence has long stood for "Learn, Share, and Grow." As an industry, manufacturers need to inculcate that thinking far beyond what we're doing with day-to-day operations. It must become part of our DNA, far beyond production. Learn, Share, and Grow is no longer an optional core competency.

The space program brought us miniaturization, the military new technologies, and governments developed the internet. The changes that products, materials, and processes are undergoing for the developed world to retain economic leadership require that type of jump-step imagination. Labor rates only define production location when products and processes allow them to.

Many people are as frustrated as I am that most universities are teaching decade(s)-old thinking and generating little meaningful knowledge. But some are doing amazing work. And some are part of innovative hubs that include businesses, research, investors, a multitude of related expertise, and knowledge capture and sharing. These hubs tend to have concentrated focus, and are becoming the most successfully innovative ensembles imaginable.

Akron, Ohio is renowned for both losing the tire business and for leading-edge materials development. Tire manufacturing is history there, but materials development is vibrant. The University of Akron became a leading research and development organization for materials under the leadership of a prior president. Now, it suffers from dysfunctional administration. The entire Akron region is vested in getting those problems solved and ensuring that the technological leadership of the school is retained.

And Akron provides but a single example of how universities, companies, local governments, and investors are slashing silos and changing the future.

Continuous improvement is a matter of necessity. Breakthrough advancements within an organization are also required. But neither is enough to stave off low labor rate countries forever. If success involves more than profits—if it also involves enriching employees, customers, suppliers, and the surrounding community—then innovation must make labor rates inconsequential to the location of production. That is done by creating products and processes that require an educated workforce and define market needs.

This approach to innovation and operations strategy does not preclude producing near your markets. The recent GE announcement that it will locate production to minimize the impact of constantly shifting political policies around the world fits fully within this thinking. In fact, not long ago GE opened a jet engine plant in the southern United States to partner with a nearby university that houses rare expertise. It's also operating production facilities elsewhere, as its financial and technological needs are met in many places beyond North America.

Operations leadership is more than a Gemba walk, though that is important. It involves ensuring product development processes that provide speed-to-market with market-verified products. It also involves looking externally to strategically position the organization for continual success. And that can't happen alone, no matter how intelligent your workforce or how strong your profits.

It's not enough to visit a neighboring plant to see their Kanban system, nor to travel to Stuttgart, Germany, to observe advanced manufacturing at its finest—though again, those expeditions can bring value. Operations leadership is responsible for providing access to processes, materials, and technologies that define the future, not reflect the past.

STRATEGY #53:

BLOCK AND TACKLE

While much has changed in our manufacturing world since the early 2000s, our objective has stayed the same: to safely provide customers what they need, when they need it, at a price that's mutually fair. Certainly the understanding of our impact on future generations has grown, and with it, our attention to resource use. Speed-to-market has always been important—but the expectation of "how fast is fast?" has changed. While the phrase "our people are our most important resource" is no more common now than it was two decades ago, more companies actually mean it now—and try to behave according to espoused values.

Each year, we have new tools and technologies and competitive pressures, but the fundamentals of success never change. As always, if you can't block and tackle, there's no reason to call the flea-flicker. Too many of us are looking for the clever, exciting path to future excellence when the most direct route starts with simply paying attention to details, and mastering the fundamentals.

Details matter. Despite employing the best American football players in the world and practicing extensively, many an NFL game is lost by a missed tackle or missed block. Whether the defense was in Cover 0 or Cover 2 doesn't really matter when a player can't make a tackle. Fundamentals matter. Paying attention to the fundamentals of manufacturing is basic to providing superior service to customers, yet often overlooked. Why? It's boring.

Ensuring master data in an ERP system is high-quality isn't nearly as exciting as developing a new product. Taking the time to understand why one component is specified over another seemingly similar one is not nearly as exciting as rolling out to new markets. Managing product life cycles is not nearly as exciting as developing a new ad campaign. Companies don't have to make a choice. Often they don't even realize that they have. They just lose focus on the fundamental details that make it all work well, chasing the next shiny object.

The newly fashionable "customer experience officer" should be spending as much time on ensuring basic processes are robust as he does on designing a new retail outlet. After all, customer loyalty still relies on "the experience," which includes accurate charges and the what/when/how many ordered being delivered as requested.

There's plenty of money wasted by ignoring the fundamentals. And as your company looks to build a bright future, you ignore the fundamentals at your own peril. Even under the bright lights of Broadway, the play has to be good.

STRATEGY #54:

INVEST IN YOUR EMPLOYEES

Who you choose to interview for open positions at your company—and why—is one of the most critical components of building a strong future for your organization. Many manufacturers believe that only an engineer can design products; only someone who's been in supply chain for 10 years can execute supply chain; and only someone with years of management experience can manage effectively. They're always looking for experience instead of for thought processes and characteristics that fit the organization's outlook for the future.

Look, I get it. It's a heck of a lot easier for managers to hire someone with 10 years of experience, who doesn't need any training, than it is to hire someone who's brand new at the job. But if you fail to look at what you'll need employees to do five years from now, and what kind of employees you want to help build your company's future, then you'll come to regret most—if not all—of your hiring decisions.

By way of example, years ago, I fell in love with a resume. I hired an Ivy League school grad with what looked like ideal experience. Unfortunately for all involved, and despite my best efforts to work with him, I had to let him go in under one year. He wasn't a bad person, and undoubtedly went on to success elsewhere. He simply didn't fit into the culture that we had created and wanted to maintain. Our replacement had half the education and experience, but had the commitment to learn and contribute to the organization well beyond his job description.

I think of that hiring error as I listen to manufacturers complain about a skill shortage that's largely self-inflicted. North American manufacturers chose to outsource, overlooking the unintended consequence of losing a skilled workforce to other industries, and making manufacturing an unattractive career choice. Now that the folly of chasing cheaper labor all over the world has been recognized, we're feeling the impact. This decade, I've seen hiring frequently become an act of desperation where an experienced body is more important than the person's potential to contribute. Such-short sighted decisions have unintended consequences, ones to be avoided.

As you now look for people to join your work teams, old job definitions and attraction and interviewing practices won't be successful. Here are five do's and don'ts to help you hire and invest in the right employees for your future:

1. Quit requiring experience in a specific set of tasks or roles.
Candidates' eagerness and ability to learn quickly means much more than experience once they're on the job. Smart engaged employees will learn the skillsets required for any job within a short period of time.

2. Quit expecting people to be willing to sit alone at a desk all day.
If you want a team instead of a department, create one. Make room for smart, energetic people who share your values, even if you don't have an opening aligned with their background. And, on a related note, never judge applicants based on their physical attire. I've seen great leadership from people with purple hair and tattoos.

3. Never stop developing your employees.
Once you have employees in your organization, develop apprenticeship roles throughout the organization, especially in skills that are difficult to build quickly. Be up front about your development processes with candidates. Qualified people with the right attitude will want to work at your organization once they hear that you're dedicated to developing existing employees.

4. Treat new hires with respect.
If you've hired wisely, your new employees have the potential to be great contributors to your organization. Boost them. Treat them with respect, starting with their first day on the job. Encourage their contributions early on, and make them feel welcome from the start. That takes more than the standard HR first-day-spiel and pointing them to a desk.

5. Quit believing that "water-cooler conversations" are equivalent to goofing off.
Let your employees talk, socialize, and take breaks together during work hours. At-work conversations are a powerful source of communication, belonging, and feeling refreshed in the work environment. Work-life balance important to all of us requires the demonstrated trust of leadership.

STRATEGY #55:

AIM FOR SUSTAINABILITY

According to the Harvard Business Review, over the last 50 years, the average lifespan of S&P 500 companies has shrunk from around 60 years to closer to 18 years. Data abounds to support the plummeting life expectancy of businesses. In this sort of climate, how can your manufacturing business aim for sustainability—and what does that truly mean?

As a small to midsized manufacturer in the U.S., these questions might knock the wind from your sails. But playing the victim doesn't change the fact that sustainability is increasingly harder to achieve. Only strategy, commitment, and action can help you get there. It's time to stand up and fight. Start by examining your business strategy with these three core questions:

1. Do your products solve a real problem that many people care about?
2. Do you have innovation and product life cycle management processes that keep your offerings relevant over time?
3. Does your business model reflect changing realities?

If you answered any of those questions with "no," government costs and automation enjoyed by your larger competitors aren't your biggest problems. Address the strategic issues immediately. Honestly assess your demonstrated commitment to operational excellence. Do you employ people capable of increasing the capabilities and productivity of your firm, or elect to hire fast and cheap? You can't be successful alone. Surround yourself with talent. And do your maintenance, onboarding, process definition, design, and quality assurance processes support enhanced productivity? If not, they should.

If you fear any necessary systemic changes are too expensive, be honest about your options. Money is easier to find than profitable ideas and superior talent. A great product with high costs and low sporadic quality won't last long. Next, be quite certain that the work employees are performing is the important work consistent with your strategy and commitment to operational excellence. Establish clear priorities that tie to visible goals and objectives, and take action.

Some manufacturers are currently well-positioned; those organizations must realize that this condition can be ephemeral, and prioritize accordingly. Others are well-positioned, and think they see the finish line. But the race never ends when it comes to sustainability. Unfortunately, many manufacturers are losing to the competition, not realizing they've already been lapped.

The odds are against any specific business surviving for multiple generations, much less thriving. To overcome those odds, robust strategy, relentless commitment to relevant excellence, and decisive action are the starting blocks. You can beat the worsening odds to become a sustainable business, but not by complaining how unfair the world is. Change it instead.

//

Money is easier to find than profitable ideas and superior talent."

STRATEGY #56:

BUILD AND MAINTAIN

In working with manufacturers over the years, I've observed that some executives are excited by the building process while others are excited by maintaining what has already been created. Thankfully, there are some who value—and can execute—both.

Neither building nor maintaining is sufficient on its own. Builders get bored when the excitement slows down, while maintainers prefer the "steady as she goes" mantra. Both have value in the right situation, but each can be disruptive in the wrong one.

I've seen good, capable leaders lose their jobs simply because their "builder mentality" wasn't a good fit anymore. It wasn't anyone's fault. These square-peg-round-hole situations are easy to spot. It's important to do so early on and constantly communicate expectations in every direction. Why? Driven, high-energy executives join a business to build processes in an organization to support growth. They lead change. They work tirelessly to move a C capability to an A, and just as tirelessly to move an A-minus to an A. Their act can get old, winning more enemies than friends. It doesn't have to, but it often does.

On the other hand, maintainers are not anti-change; they are simply more focused on stabilizing the current condition, and then leading select changes in a very controlled manner. In an urgent scenario, maintainers seem un-leader-like. They're criticized for moving too slowly. They have no sense of urgency, yet they're focused on making sure the dam is strong before adding more water behind it.

The best operations leaders are those who recognize when the organization needs to exhale, and lets it take a quick breath before leading the next charge. Those who know that constant change can destabilize prior improvements. Those who know that nothing happens without the buy-in of people. They take time to ensure common goals. They know there's only one speed in our worldwide economy—and that's "faster." If you only look for a sense of urgency in your operations leadership, you might get just that. If you only look for a steady hand, you might get just that. What most companies need is someone who can provide both, that type of leadership that can ensure a steady yet fast moving growth-oriented future.

Remember, Apple got tired of the unwavering genius of Steve Jobs and fired him. Years later, the board decided he was exactly what they needed and brought him back. Meeting short-term needs with someone who also meets your organization's long-term vision and values—now, that's ideal. If you can't recognize or find that, don't be surprised when you need to make another leadership change.

STRATEGY #57:

ASSESS YOUR CAPABILITIES

Some market shifts are easily handled, but some can break an entire supply chain. The purpose of assessing your capabilities is to ensure a current and accurate perception of what kind of market shifts you can handle—and which mutations require investment of time, money, and new capabilities. Without a formal process for assessing the boundaries of your current capabilities, you'll eventually be caught unaware and left behind.

So how do you design and execute this capabilities assessment process to ensure that it's valuable? Here are three key steps:

1. Establish a strong risk management process.
2. Utilize scenario planning to identify potential weak points.
3. Develop a sensitivity analysis tool to reflect conditions over time.

For example, what if sales were to double in the next 12 months? Where would your operational performance be stressed? Which processes aren't scalable?

Now, a different situation. What if your product mix reversed its current ratio? Which equipment, tooling, and materials would immediately become bottlenecks?

Consider a broad spectrum of 10 to 15 scenarios, identifying the components, the equipment, the tooling, the manpower, the financials, perhaps the software, the suppliers and other key contributors to your current capabilities that would be on the critical path.

It sounds like a lot, but it's not bad at all. Identify cause triggers that would immediately necessitate an assessment and quite likely action to ameliorate deterioration in your operational strength. This doesn't need to be fancy. It does need to be practical, however. And it needs to be sufficiently representative to spot trouble before it hits.

It's vital to challenge your traditional thinking when preparing for the future in this way. Unexpected market shifts can and do happen. The best companies already know how to respond. This process must be integrated with your sales and operations planning, and your strategic processes. Then listen carefully for potential changes that could impact the model or your triggers.

What we can assuredly predict is volatility. That means we must position our businesses to quickly and effectively change course multiple times, and we must know when to act. Moving any business forward requires conviction, even in turbulent conditions. Conviction, however, does not mean disregard for the possibilities.

Bad decisions are never appropriate. If you can't swim, don't dive into the deep end. But even if you can, you never want to dive into the shallow end. If you're not sure of the depth, get data. Never swim alone. And before you get wet, confirm that the water is the best of alternative paths. Succeeding in volatile times is really no different than during stable periods.

Ford's recent decision to close its Indonesian and Japanese operations reflects rational stop-loss to the prior horrible decision to put them there. None of the reasons given for poor performance in those markets is news. While demographics and economics suggested many car buyers, nothing suggested they would buy Fords. And they didn't. Every business makes bad decisions. The responsibility of leadership is to limit their number and impact, and to learn lessons when they happen. Signing long-term contracts with volume guarantees is risky in the best of times. After all, the best of times don't last forever. A long-term contract specifying a percentage of demand is more flexible. If you need to scale your supply chain either up or down, understand and document the variables involved in reversing course with minimal pain to all parties.

This isn't pushing risk onto others, nor is it a lack of conviction. It's sharing important information to enable risk management by all. The Gambler tells us: "If you're gonna play the game, boy, you gotta learn to play it right."

Regardless of the volatility you suspect, always identify the assumptions that are most critical to the success of a decision, and those most likely to be wrong. It may be riskier to do nothing than to make the change you're considering, so be sure to include that possibility as well.

Identify trigger points for those key assumptions, at which time you will reassess your decision. You can choose to limit your investment, or to double down.

If you don't recognize the critical assumptions or the trigger points, invest more in understanding the options and potential outcomes. When a trigger point is reached, stick with facts, not hopes. I've seen too many companies discount triggers because they simply wanted too much to believe.

Once in a rare while we get totally blindsided, but it's much more common to find that an important assumption was misguided. So whether you're nervous about this next year, or confident, listen to the Gambler. Learn to play it right.

STRATEGY #58:

LOOK PAST THE HORIZON

An IndustryWeek article featured a number of manufacturing companies that have been in existence since the 1800s, supplemented by relative newcomers—those created shortly after 1900. What separates these businesses from the multitudes that have come and gone in the last decade, much less the last 50 years? Look at the names: Procter and Gamble, Johnson & Johnson, Timken, Goodyear, and Merck. Companies that have had an unwavering commitment to the customer, to their credo, and to constantly improving their products and services. Companies that win competitions for "best company to work for."

Each of these companies has struggled at times, but they didn't take tempting shortcuts. Johnson & Johnson's handling of the Tylenol scandal is still held as the gold standard for how to handle a perceived quality problem when customers are at risk. The reluctance of some auto manufacturers to recall known quality problems lies in stark contrast. If you want to be included on IndustryWeek's list in the year 2100, look past the horizon to consider the following prerequisites:

1. Have a mission and vision and company credo that has real meaning and guides decision-making during the most challenging of times.
2. Reliably do what's right for your customers, even when the customers aren't right.
3. Treat your employees like they're your most valuable asset. Because they are.

Let me give you a real-life example of a company that learned to look past the horizon, after facing the consequences of being unprepared for an unexpected future. Several years ago, I stood in the office of a VP of global operations looking at a graph on his wall. The VP stood next to me, explaining the data. The company had been hit hard by the most recent downturn and shutting the supply chain down had been messy and expensive.

After years of growing, they simply had been unprepared for the precipitous fall in sales they experienced. Our conversation was not about that, but about how to better predict when to begin to open the supply chain faucets again. We both knew that off-on wouldn't work. A planned and gradual return would be necessary.

The billion-dollar company was required by its board of directors to use a common forecasting source, one that had been fairly good, but always a few months late predicting turns. The question: How could we comply with that directive and still not get caught behind the eight-ball once again?

We developed a low-risk plan to selectively meet with key suppliers and their suppliers to understand the challenges they would face when increasing volumes. We examined internal capacity limiters and developed triggers to flag when decision time was fast approaching. A few strategic investments and purchases were planned and then slowly executed to balance the risk of doing nothing—and of doing too much, too soon.

As is often the case, the forecast reported the upturn in the economy a few months after it really began. Based on it, the multi-level plan already in place was gradually released. The company's doing quite well now. A supplier capacity planning and analysis team has processes in place to predict and address challenges of additional growth, or decline. Internal triggers have proven very effective and are regularly reviewed. The VP that I met with has since retired, but now I'm scheduled to meet with his replacement. Our conversation? Planning for the next unexpected change of pace, whether up or down.

While individual contributors are handling day-to-day operations and mid-level managers are ensuring that near-turn plans are sufficient and continuing to focus on process improvements, the leadership team must be looking at the next great opportunity both to succeed and to fail. Look past the horizon to ensure that, short of worldwide calamity, you can smoothly adjust the supply chain, product development and life cycle management, and financial realities while maintaining your company's vision and core values.

WHAT'S JUST OVER THE HORIZON FOR YOU?

ABOUT THE AUTHOR

Rebecca A. Morgan is the president of Fulcrum ConsultingWorks, Inc., a Cleveland, Ohio-based operations consulting company. Since 1990, Morgan has positioned scores of manufacturers for long-term success, helping them build resources and capabilities that are leveraged for maximum advantage. Morgan's typical clients are manufacturers with sales ranging from $200 million to $1 billion; Fortune Brands, Avery-Dennison, VitaMix, and Hunter Defense Technologies are just a few of the many companies that have turned to Morgan's expertise over the years.

Growing and processing poultry. Forecasting interest rates. Making macaroni and cheese. Producing state-of-the-art blades and vanes for the high temperature/high pressure sections of jet engines. Rebecca Morgan succeeded in each of these industries as she quickly learned how to see and leverage commonalities and distinctions. Following those 14 years in the corporate world, she has spent the past 26 years helping manufacturers grow and succeed in a broad spectrum of operational environments. Process, discrete, and job shops. Consumer and industrial. Chemicals, metals, plastics, rubber, electronics, precious stones, ceramics, assembly, and more. And she loves them all!

Morgan is committed to helping manufacturers develop capabilities to profitably deliver competitive advantage, brand promise, and customer loyalty. She not only helps others do it, but she's done it herself. Before founding Fulcrum, she served in leadership at Perdue Farms, Cleveland Trust, Stouffer Foods, TRW, and Precision CastParts.

As a member of Stouffer's management team, Morgan led and coordinated operations support to Stouffer Foods' introduction of the wildly successful Lean Cuisine brand (demand exceeded forecast by an order of magnitude) while contributing to product and distribution rationalization associated with construction of a second plant.

Following that, Morgan helped prepare TRW's then $300 million casting division for sale, subsequently playing a key leadership role for Precision CastParts in the turnaround of that acquisition.

Before Stouffers, as bank economist for Cleveland Trust (since acquired by Key Bank), she stood with an exceptionally small group who forecast the 20 percent prime interest rate that few thought could happen, but soon did. Even earlier at Perdue Farms, Morgan led development and implementation of decision support processes and accounting systems.

During that same time, she was an adjunct assistant professor of Economics at Salisbury State University.

Morgan holds bachelor's and master's degrees in economics, and completed post-graduate work in business administration. She is board-approved in operations management by the Society for Advancement of Consulting, certified as a fellow by The Association for Operations Management, and was awarded lifetime member status of the Association of Manufacturing Excellence.

Morgan is a contributing manufacturing operations expert writer for IndustryWeek, American City Business Journals, and AME's Target. The highly respected business journal INC Magazine also selected Morgan as its operations expert, a role she filled for several years. In addition, Morgan's expertise is frequently featured by other national and industry publications, including the Wall Street Journal, Fortune, Business Week, and Dow-Jones Newswires, as well as by various radio programs.

While accomplishing all that, she always makes time for sports, motorcycle riding, and world-wide travel. Work-life balance is her existence, not just a goal.

TESTIMONIALS

"Becky helped us evolve our organization, develop our operations strategy and make it actionable so we could turn it into real results. Becky has been a real asset to us and I really appreciate her."
—Joe Pullella, VP Manufacturing, VitaMix Corp

"If you are truly ready to have an objective mirror held up against the state of your manufacturing operations, along with the deep commitment required to march on the path of continuous improvement, Becky is the resource you should use. She not only gets to the root of your issues, she remains engaged throughout the process to help resolve them."
—Vince Slusarz, COO, Kinetico, Inc.

"I highly recommend Becky to help with any manufacturing-related issues. I hired her, and was amazed how she was able to come in to a manufacturing plant and quickly identify opportunities to improve efficiency and fix problems. Her insight was fantastic and her services were a great investment."
—Jon Hedges, GM, SuperTrapp Industries

"Becky stands apart from the myriad business, productivity, lean, and operations consultants. Becky brings first-rate skills to every engagement. Her personal work experience in operations coupled with her passion for continuous learning & growth make her the equivalent of several different consultants. Becky's integrity and dedication to each client make her special."
—Brian Fink, VP Operations, Mantaline

"I had the opportunity to work with Becky while re-designing the organization and processes of a traditional Materials organization to one with responsibility and accountability. Becky was a tremendous help when I was working on an organizational redesign and work flows. Becky is a first class business professional and always focused on the

business objectives of the customer. She has the unique ability to bridge the gap between; service consultancy, the needs and expectations of client Management and those of the end user. Becky always worked toward a win win for client Management and the end user. Class A performer"
—Art Koch, Director Supply Chain, Avery-Dennison

"Becky did an excellent job putting together a great strategic direction for our quality systems and I would recommend hiring her."
—Paul Calaway, Director, Operations & Supply Chain Beckett Gas

"Becky is someone I have known and admired for a very long time. She'll stop and ask 'who are you, culturally where have you come from, where do you want to go,' so she can ensure your introduction starts in a manner befitting all that. Our journey has been very successful so far and I attribute a lot of that to the fact that we started right. If you're thinking about Lean, you should think about Becky."
—Ronne Proche, President & CEO, Zircoa

"Becky was instrumental in giving us a roadmap to make our company a better company. She was a pleasure to work with."
—Gary Davis, President, Aetna Plastics

"We expect, as we continue to follow the principles that Becky has instilled in our organization, we will continue to see greater profits. I would recommend her to anyone."
—Eric Laker, Owner, Lashbrook

"Becky's skills and depth of knowledge have helped our company realize our goals. We have had and continue to have success as a result of the great advice and guidance that Becky has provided."
—Wendy Wloszek, President, Industrial Mold & Machine

"We hired Becky to help us reduce inventory and improve quality and space utilization. She helped us convert to cells and left us with the knowledge of how to do that."
—Annette Dockus, VP, Operations, Superior Tool Company

ACKNOWLEDGMENTS

My life began on "the wrong side of the tracks" but progressed to success in every measure I hold dear. Without the example of my parents' dedication to hard work and my brother Bob's suggestion I consider economics courses in college, this journey would have been quite different. I learned how to think, how to make short-term sacrifices for long-term gain, and that it's quite all right to simply not know, as long as I keep searching for important answers.

Sincere thanks to all those who exposed me to the wonderful world of manufacturing and the field of operations, and to those who subsequently invited me to help make their companies better.

And thank you to Chad Barr for continuously encouraging me to write this book, and to Stephanie Mann for making it more readable.

Several strategies in this book draw from my own articles that were previously published in various publications. Thanks to those publications for their permission to reprint the content in this book. In particular, Strategies #20, #25, #37, and #52 include my articles that were previously published in AME's Target; Strategies #38, #39, #42, #45, #52, #53, and #55 include those that were previously published in IndustryWeek; and Strategies #45 and #57 include those that were previously published in American City Business Journals.

www.fulcrumcwi.com

Fulcrum ConsultingWorks, Inc.

Adress: 17204 Dorchester Drive
Cleveland, OH 44119-1302
USA

Phone: (216) 486-9570

General email: info@fulcrumcwi.com

Via Social Media:

http://twitter.com/fulcrumcwi

https://www.facebook.com
/fulcrumcwi

http://www.linkedin.com/in
/beckymorganfulcrum

Rebecca Morgan

35906434R00098

Made in the USA
Middletown, DE
18 October 2016